EFFORT-LESS WEALTH

EFFORT-LESS WEALTH

Smart Money Strategies for Every Stage of Your Life
(Getting Rich Does Not Have To Be Hard)

By Tom Corley
With Tom Haughey

MCP BOOKS

MCP Books
2301 Lucien Way #415
Maitland, FL 32751
407.339.4217
www.millcitypress.net

Printed in the United States of America

ISBN-13: 978-1-5456-8106-0
LCCN: 2020900060

Table of Contents

About the Author ix

Acknowledgements xi

Introduction xv

JC's Plan 1

Meet the Neighbors 5

Engagement Stage 15

Wedding Stage 21

Honeymoon Stage 31

First Apartment Stage 39

Saving For First Home Stage 43

Home Purchase Stage 51

Growing Family Stage 59

Home Improvements Stage 65

The Savings Mindset 75

Child Education Stage 83

Career Management Stage 89

Life's Unexpected Consequences 95

College and Retirement Stages 99

JC Job's Smart Money Principles 103

ADVANCED PRAISE

"Tom Corley's passion for his subject shines through in this book. His ingenious idea of weaving his Smart Money Principles into an educational and fun read, helps to bring the habits of good money management to life,"
- Kate Williams, Rich Habits Blog subscriber.

"Tom Corley's book, Effort-Less Wealth, is both practical AND interesting! He brings to life, in a concise story, the ongoing lessons from his daily blogs – which folks of ALL ages would benefit from."
- John Garner, Rich Habits Blog subscriber

"As a healthcare professional, I thoroughly enjoy Tom Corley's work, as it combines brain science, health habits and wealth creation, all in one."
- Mario Cocco

"I'm sooooo lovin' this book."
- Bambi Blount, Rich Habits blog subscriber.

"I think Effort-Less Wealth is a great educational book that is easy and fun to read. It is packed with extremely valuable lessons."
- Ajay Jani, Rich habits Blog subscriber.

About the Author

 Tom is a bestselling and award winning author. His books include: *Rich Habits, Rich Kids, Change Your Habits Change Your Life and Rich Habits Poor Habits.* Tom has appeared on or in CBS Evening News, The Dave Ramsey Show, CNN, MSN Money, USA Today, the Huffington Post, Marketplace Money, SUCCESS Magazine, Inc. Magazine, Reader's Digest, Money Magazine, Kiplinger's Personal Finance Magazine, Fast Company Magazine, Epoca Magazine (Brazil's largest weekly) and thousands of other media outlets in the U.S. and 25 other countries. Tom is a frequent contributor to Business Insider, CNBC and other national media outlets.

Tom Corley is an internationally recognized authority on habits and wealth creation. He has traveled the world speaking to thousands in Australia, Canada, the United States and Vietnam. His inspiring keynote addresses cover success habits of the rich, failure habits of the poor, the four paths to creating wealth and cutting edge habit change strategies.

Tom has spoken alongside Richard Branson, Mark Victor Hansen, Robin Sharma, Dr. Daniel Amen and many other notable speakers.

In Tom's five-year study of the rich and poor, he identified over 300 daily habits that separated the "haves" from the "have not's." Tom is also a CPA, CFP, holds a Master's Degree in Taxation and heads Cerefice & Company a CPA firm in New Jersey.

Acknowledgements

I owe a great deal of thanks to my childhood friend, Tom Haughey. Tom was instrumental in helping me develop the Rich Neighbor character. Tom, like myself, was born and raised on Staten Island, a borough of New York City. His dad was a New York City public school teacher in the days when teachers did not make much money. His mom was a homemaker, so raising five children on one teacher's salary meant a life of financial struggle for the family.

Tom had scripted out a life plan, but struggling financially wasn't part of that plan. Here was Tom's life plan:

- Go to college and major in accounting.
- Get straight As in college.
- Work at a prestigious CPA firm until he accumulated enough money to fund law school.
- Pass the rigorous CPA exam, while working at a prestigious CPA firm.
- Go to law school.
- Get straight As in law school.
- Work for a prestigious New York City law firm.
- Pass the bar exam, while working at a prestigious New York City law firm.
- Secure a high-paying job at a large, multi-national, publicly-held company.

Since neither he nor his family had any money, paying for college fell entirely on Tom's shoulders.

To that end, Tom worked six days a week as a lifeguard during the summer of his high school and college years. Tom saved almost all of his summer earnings, enabling him to pay for college. To minimize his costs, Tom lived at home and commuted every day to St. John's University, while many of his wealthier friends left home for college. His thrift enabled him to graduate from college debt-free.

After graduating college, Tom took a job at Arthur Andersen in New York City. Arthur Andersen, at the time, was the most prestigious CPA firm in the world. While working as an auditor at Arthur Andersen, Tom continued to live at home, commuted to New York City every day, and saved most of his income in the meantime. Tom left Andersen after three years and headed off to NYU School of Law. Despite Tom's frugal living, he ran out of money after his first year of law school and was forced to borrow $60,000 to cover the remaining two years. Sixty-thousand dollars, back then, is approximately $120,000 in today's dollars, a significant sum. Upon graduating NYU, Tom secured a job at a very prestigious law firm in New York City. After a number of years, Tom left the law firm and entered the corporate world, where he would work for a number of large publicly-held, multinational companies, as a corporate attorney. Tom rose the corporate ladder and became senior pharmaceutical executive at a large pharmaceutical company in New Jersey, helping them navigate through a number of company restructurings and was financially rewarded for his efforts.

Acknowledgements

Tom and his wife, Margaret, were diligent savers and frugal with their money. They eschewed private schools and country clubs to diligently save and prudently invest their savings. They were able to send all three of their children to Dartmouth, a very prestigious and expensive Ivy League school, thanks to the 529 College Savings Plans they had funded for each child. At age fifty-two, Tom retired a self-made millionaire. Because Tom possessed many of the Rich Habits that I uncovered in my five-year *Rich Habits Study*, I decided to build my Rich Neighbor character around his life story.

Introduction

When I travel the country speaking to high school and college students about exactly what they need to do to become financially successful in life, I always begin my presentation by asking three questions:

"How many want to be financially successful in life?"

"How many think they will be financially successful in life?"

Almost every time I ask the first two questions, every hand rises in the air. Then I ask the magic third question:

"How many have taken a course in school on how to be financially successful in life?"

Not one hand rises in the air, ever, with this last question. Clearly every student wants to be successful and thinks he/she will be successful, but none have been taught by their parents or their teachers how. Not only are there no courses on basic financial success principles available in schools, there are few, if any, structured courses teaching basic money management, anywhere. We are raising our children to be financially illiterate and to fail in life.

Is it any wonder that most people live paycheck to paycheck? That most accumulate more debt than assets and many lose their homes when they lose their job? Is it any wonder that most people in the industrialized world cannot afford college for their children?

For five years, I studied the daily habits of 233 millionaires (177 were self-made millionaires) in order to find out what they were doing right. I also studied the daily habits of 128 individuals, struggling in poverty, in order to find out what they were doing wrong. I've shared these Rich Habits and Poor Habits with over 100 million people around the world through thousands of media interviews and various books–*Rich Habits, Rich Kids, Change Your Habits Change Your Life and Rich Habits Poor Habits*. Most of my books have become huge bestsellers, with *Rich Kids* even winning a number of literary awards. As a result, I've become a well-known habits and wealth expert, not only in the U.S., but around the world.

My goal in writing this book is to share the smart money habits you need to have, at each stage of your life, in order to accumulate the wealth you will need to be financially free. I know these smart money habits work because I've received thousands of letters, emails, cards and social media posts from my readers and followers over the years, thanking me for helping them rise from poverty or the middle-class, transforming not only their lives but the lives of their children. You see, the wealth-building strategies you will learn in this book will also benefit your children and their children. Future generations will have you to thank for teaching them the financial success habits that I learned from my *Rich Habits* research.

I don't want to mislead you, building wealth can be very hard. It all depends on the path you choose in creating the wealth you need in order to become financially free. From my *Rich Habit*s research, I found there are four very different paths towards accumulating wealth:

Hardest Path to Building Wealth–The Dreamer/ Entrepreneur Path

Pursuing a dream can be the most rewarding thing you ever do, not only in terms of personal fulfillment but also in terms of financial success. The Dreamer/Entrepreneurs in my study loved what they did for a living and that passion showed up in their bank accounts. This group of self-made millionaires had an average Net Worth of $7.4 million, far more than any other group of millionaires in my study. But that higher wealth came at a cost.

Costs of being a Dreamer/Entrepreneur:
- Long Work Hours – The Dreamer/Entrepreneurs in my study worked an average of 61 hours a week, for twelve years. Weekend and vacations were almost non-existent. Those long work hours impacted everyone in the Dreamer's immediate orbit. Family and friends are hit the hardest by their absence. Often one spouse must take up the slack and raise their children, almost as if they were a single parent. Close friendships whither on the vine, due to those long work hours.
- Financial Stress – Until the Dream begins to pay off, making ends meet can cause almost intolerable stress. Only the strong can survive that stress and that includes the spouses. In the early going, getting a steady paycheck is near impossible. Weak marriages will almost certainly fall apart, due to this stress.

- **High Risk** – Dreamers have to put everything they own on the line. Their homes, retirement plans, and savings become the assets that breathes life into their Dream. When a Dreamer runs out of assets, they have no choice but to turn to debt in order to continue to finance their Dream. The lucky ones are eventually able to secure Lines of Credit to keep them afloat. The unlucky ones are forced to rely on credit cards or loans from family and friends to survive until they thrive. If they thrive. Pursuing a Dream is a gamble. There's absolutely no guarantee that the Dream will every pay off. Many fail. In fact, 27% in my Rich Habits Study failed at least once. Failure can mean bankruptcy. Sometimes that bankruptcy is followed by divorce.

Second Hardest Path to Building Wealth–The Big Company Climber Path

Climbers are individuals who work for a big company and spend their entire careers climbing the company ladder until they reach the upper echelons – senior executive status. In my *Rich Habits Study*, it took Climbers about 22 years to accumulate an average Net Worth of $3.4 million. Much of that wealth came from either stock compensation or a partnership share of profits.

Costs of being a Climber:
- **Long Work Hours** – Like the Dreamers, Climbers have to work long hours. Most Climbers have to travel regularly. Airports, hotel rooms and taxis

become a way of life. And very often, Climbers have to work during weekends and on vacations.

- Political Expertise – Besides the hard work, Climbers must possess expert political skills. Those who do are able to outmaneuver their internal competitors–other Climbers, biting at their heels and stabbing them in the back, as opportunities present themselves. There is always some other Climber seeking to undermine you in order to advance their personal agenda, which is usually the same as yours–climbing further up the company ladder.

- Power Relationships – Climbers need mad relationship-building skills. Those who succeed in reaching the upper echelons of a big company are almost certainly the best at building relationships, both within the organization they work for and within their industry. Building these strong, powerful relationships, however, takes time, energy and money. Frequent phone calls, constant entertainment, attending weddings, birthday parties or funerals and sending thoughtful cards for special occasions. Just managing all of those Power Relationships can take up a big part of your workday.

- Risk – Like the Dreamer Path, the Climber Path has some unique risks. If the company struggles financially, for whatever reason, your time investment in that company may not be rewarded, to the extent you expected.

Third Hardest Path to Building Wealth – The Virtuoso Path

When you are a Virtuoso, it means you are among the top experts in your industry or field. That expertise may be knowledge-based or skill-based. Virtuosos are paid a high premium for their expertise. That high premium means they are able to earn more money than their non-Virtuoso peers.

Costs of being a Virtuoso:

- Significant Investment – Becoming a Virtuoso requires an enormous investment in time, and often money. Knowledge-based Virtuosos spend many years in continuous study. Oftentimes, this requires formal education, such as advanced degrees (PhD, Medical Degrees, Law Degrees, etc.). Skill-based Virtuosos devote themselves to many years of deliberate practice and analytical practice. Deliberate practice requires thousands of hours honing your skills. Analytical practice often requires the services of a coach, mentor or expert who can provide immediate feedback. This feedback, in most cases, costs money.
- Long Hours – Like the Dreamer and Climber, the Virtuoso has to work long hours, not only in perfecting their knowledge or skills, but also in maintaining and using them. Virtuosos are rare and, therefore, in high demand. That high demand means many long hours serving the needs of others in exchange for money.

Easiest Path to Building Wealth – The Saver-Investor Path

What if I told you that there is an easy, guaranteed way to accumulate wealth? There is a path to becoming a self-made millionaire that does not require any unique set of skills, special knowledge, taking significant risks or long, oppressive work hours, isolating you from your family and friends.

The Saver-Investor Path is not only the easiest path to building wealth, it is also the guaranteed path to building wealth. But this easy, guaranteed path does have four requirements:

1. Middle-Class Income – It's hard to save when you are poor. Most of the poor are barely able to meet the costs of even a low standard of living. But, if you have a middle-class income and keep your standard of living low, this will give you the ability to save.

2. Discipline – The typical Saver-Investor saves 20% or more of their income and lives off what's left. This requires discipline in saving first and discipline in minimizing how much money you spend.

3. Consistency – Saver-Investors consistently save and consistently invest their savings so that their wealth can grow every year.

4. Time – The typical Saver-Investor consistently saved and prudently invested their savings over an average of 32 years.

In my *Rich Habits Study* the Saver-Investors accumulated an average of $3.3 million. This path requires that you start early–almost immediately upon entering the adult work force. If you start later in life, and still desire to retire wealthy, you will have to increase your savings rate by 10% for every ten years you failed to save. And you will have to work longer. For example, if you decide to pursue the Saver-Investor Path in your mid-thirties, you will have to increase your annual saving to 30% of your net income and work into your mid-sixties. If you start in your mid-forties, you will have to increase your annual savings to 40% of net income and work into your mid-seventies.

Everyone's life is a series of stages: childhood, primary school, secondary school, college for some, getting your first apartment, marriage, starting a family, buying your first family home, managing your growing family, balancing work and family while managing your career, empty nest stage and finally, the retirement stage. Money mistakes you make in one stage can have a ripple effect, impacting one or more subsequent stages. Make too many money mistakes, in any stage, and you will find yourself in perpetual catch-up mode, the rest of your adult life.

Those who make the right decisions at every stage, prime themselves for financial success. In this book, I will show you exactly what you should be doing at every stage of your life to achieve financial success.

The foundation for sound financial decisions are smart money habits. When you have smart money habits, you are able to save and invest during each stage of your life. This is so that when your kids leave the nest or you enter your retirement stage, you are free from financial worries and not financially dependent on your children or loved ones.

Financial success is a process. Understanding and following that process, virtually guarantees that you will become, at the very least, financially independent and, perhaps, even wealthy.

In this book, I will share with you that process, embodied by specific smart money habits for each stage of your life.

By following the lessons in this book, you will immediately catapult yourself into the top five percent of individuals – the five percent who never have to worry about having enough money.

JC's Plan

The Jersey Shore is a magical place. There is nothing quite like it in the world. One hundred and thirty miles of coastline, spanning from Sandy Hook to Cape May. Its unmatched beaches boast beautiful barrier islands and bays adorned with majestic lighthouses, quaint fishing villages and an assortment of eccentric jetties that separate one beach from the next; some with wooden piers that seem to go on forever and others fabricated with mammoth boulders, intimidating the most energetic of waves. Perhaps the most unique aspect of the Jersey Shore beaches are the distinct boardwalks. Each beach parades its boardwalk as though it were a peacock displaying its magnificent feathers, in an effort to compete for the affection of the many beach lovers who descend upon the Jersey Shore every summer.

JC Jobs was excited because his son had just dropped off three of JC's grandkids at his home in Manasquan Beach. They were going to spend the entire month of July with him and this made him happy. All three were the perfect age, in JC's mind, for some mentoring. Casey, the youngest, was twelve. Kirsten was thirteen. Brendan, the oldest, had just turned fifteen. They all worshiped JC and loved hearing his stories. And JC had many stories.

JC was world famous. His self-help, success books had sold over half a billion copies world-wide. His devoted readers included a Who's Who list of presidents, senators, kings, princes, CEOs, self-made millionaires, Hollywood actors and actresses, notable teachers, religious leaders, business owners and professionals in every field imaginable. Organizations paid him $10,000 just to have him speak, which was a lot of money to pay a speaker back in 1985. Even at age sixty-nine, JC was as busy as he'd ever been. Flying around the world to share his research and his lessons, took up a great deal of his time. Plus, JC continued to update his research and write new books every year, sharing his success research.

But, when it came to his grandkids, JC had all of the time in the world. He was devoted to teaching them and mentoring them to be the best they possibly could be. And to do that, JC had a plan in mind, or rather an adventure. He and his three grandkids would embark on a very ambitious journey–a month-long assault of the beaches at the Jersey Shore.

"I've got quite an adventure in store for us," JC beamed as his grandkids made their way from their station wagon to his house. JC hurriedly ushered them into his dining room, upon which sat a map so large it took up the entire eight-foot-long table.

"What's that?" Casey asked JC, squinting her eyes to see the map more clearly.

"It's a map of every beach in New Jersey," JC replied with a mischievous smile.

"Why do you have it out on the dining room table?" Brendan asked.

"I told you. I have an adventure in store for us," JC said, shrugging his shoulders nonchalantly.

"What adventure?" Casey begged.

JC had mapped out twelve of the best beaches the Jersey Shore had to offer. He told his grandkids that the plan was to spend a few days at his Manasquan home, and then the following week they would all pile into JC's RV, working their way from one beach to the next. The excitement grew on their faces as JC went into more detail about their journey.

"I figure once we leave Manasquan, it will take us about a month to hit all of these beaches. We'll spend at least one day at every beach and sleep in the RV at night. We'll visit their boardwalks, buy boardwalk stuff, play board-walk games, and eat boardwalk food. We'll take in every activity each beach has to offer and wring the fun out of every beach, one by one." JC smiled a devilish smile as his grandkids jumped around like Mexican jumping beans, in anticipation of all the fun they knew they were about to experience with JC over the next month.

Meet the Neighbors

Their trip officially began at Manasquan Beach, JC's home beach. Manasquan's boardwalk was one of a kind. It was the only one at the Jersey Shore not made of wood. In reality, it wasn't a boardwalk at all, but rather a half mile-long concrete path that ran parallel to the water, separating First Avenue and the sand. Dozens of merchants set up shop along First Avenue. You could buy surf boards, bathing suits, inflatable tubes, flip flops and pretty much anything you would need for your beach vacation. Those shops came in handy as the group spent the next two days buying everything under the sun they thought might be needed for their beach journey. Kites, flip flops, T-shirts, beach pales and small shovels, so JC could dig his big, signature holes in the sand for his grandkids. They bought silicone spray, which JC used to fortify his amazing sand castles. They bought puzzles, books to read, sun screen lotion, new beach chairs, a huge beach umbrella, and the biggest beach blanket the kids had ever seen. JC even found this outrageous beach wagon that they would use to transport their beach equipment from the RV to each beach.

Once they were finished shopping, they spent a few days visiting the arcades that dotted First Avenue. JC loved seeing the little happy faces of his grandkids as they made their way along the boardwalk, visiting one arcade after another. He'd buy them whatever their little hearts desired: hermit crabs for Casey, ice cream for Kirsten and a football for Brendan. JC always got an earful from their parents, for spoiling them, but they were particularly annoyed at the hermit crabs, whose life expectancy never lasted for more than a few days once Casey took them home. Nonetheless, they were JC's for the next month and JC intended to show them the time of their lives.

One of the hallmarks that made JC 'JC' was his appetite for competition. JC loved competing with his grandkids on some of the boardwalk games, like the shoot-the-ducks game or the fill-the-balloon-with-water race. JC would get the kids all riled up as they made their way from one game to another by telling them how badly he was going to beat them. JC would get far ahead of them in those games but, magically, they always seemed to be able to pull ahead of JC at the very last moment. JC would feign anger, throwing down his gun or pistol and screaming at the arcade employee that the game was rigged or his gun was broken. The kids would always hoot and holler back at JC, calling him a sore loser. For everyone, it was not just a little slice of the Jersey Shore—it was a little slice of JC heaven.

When they were sufficiently exhausted from the boardwalk games, they headed to the RV and together they loaded the beach wagon to spend the remainder of the day on the beach.

"JC, tell us again about how Grandma came to you in a dream?" Casey asked while she, Brendan and Kirsten sat in their beach chairs, eyes riveted on JC. Since his grandkids were born, they called him JC and not Grandpa. He permitted it and even liked it. It made him feel kind of unique …. and also, not old.

JC leaned back in his chair, staring out at the rolling waves as they caressed the shoreline and took a long drag on his big, fat cigar, then exhaled. "Your grandmother loved the Jersey Shore. It was her dream that your dad, and your two aunts might grow up down the shore. Unfortunately, the money I made from my small CPA business back in 1957 put the Jersey Shore out of reach for our family. Then your grandma got cancer. When she died, your dad was just a boy, five years old. I was so mad at myself at the time. If I had only been better at making and saving money as an accountant we might have had enough money for Grandma to get the medical procedure when she needed it, instead of having to wait until the end of my very busy tax season, when we'd have the money for the operation. After tax season, Grandma went in for the procedure but it was too late–she passed away a few months later. It sent me into a downward spiral of depression that lasted a full year. At my lowest point, one night, Grandma came to me in a dream."

"What did she say, JC?" Kirsten interrupted, even though his grandkids had heard the story a hundred times before and already knew what happened.

"She said, 'All you need to do is to ask the right questions'–I didn't understand what it meant at the time but it stuck in my head. Not long after, I felt the strange need to interview rich people and poor people, in order to better understand what made the rich, rich and what made the poor, poor. So, I interviewed 233 rich people and 128 poor

7

people about their lives. I spent nearly four years asking them 144 questions each. I wanted to know what they did from the moment they put their feet on the floor in the morning to the moment they put their head on the pillow at night. I was in search of truth. I wanted to find out why so many people like me struggled financially, while others were able to accumulate enormous wealth. My hope was that if I could uncover that truth, I could then help others pull themselves out of their financial distress, so they would be able to afford *their* medical procedure for *their* spouses.

"To my great surprise, my research revealed that the cause of poverty and wealth was something as simple as your daily habits. I learned that there were specific daily habits that lifted people up financially and specific daily habits that dragged people down financially. I began to adopt many of those *Rich Habits*, that's what I called them. And my life slowly turned around: I started making and saving more money and I became much healthier. It took time, but everything started to change. In 1965, after a few years of following the *Rich Habits* and teaching them to others, I decided to write a book so I could share my research with the world. I called the book *Rich Habits*. I ended up selling close to a hundred million copies or that book. Those *Rich Habits* changed my life. And now, here we sit on the beach in Manasquan. How ironic that Grandma's death would be the thing that got us all to the Jersey Shore. Your grandma would have loved seeing your dad and aunts grow up here in Manasquan."

JC teared up. His grandkids sprung out of their beach chairs, blanketing JC with hugs and kisses. JC wiped away the tears and composed himself before resuming his story.

"Manasquan is a very special place, thanks in large part to the Manasquan River inlet. The inlet became permanent in 1931 when the US Army Corps of Engineers dredged it and placed massive bulkheads along its sides, transforming what was once a narrow, shallow inlet into a deep and wide major thoroughfare for boats. As word spread, the inlet became a major revenue-generating asset for the town, attracting thousands of fisherman and boaters from not only New Jersey but as far north as New York City and its suburbs. Eventually, many of those summer vacationers fell in love with Manasquan and started buying summer homes here. Back in 1967, new homes were popping up all over the place. Mine was one of those early new homes, ten blocks from the beach. Because my home was ten blocks from the beach, flooding wasn't an issue, so the new homes on my block were all built with full-sized basements, something the older homes didn't have.

"A few months after we moved in, two other families followed. The O'Neills to the right and the Veblens to the left. Tom O'Neill was a successful attorney with a wife and three kids. Their kids were about the same age as your dad and your aunts. Tom was also a CPA, like me. He got his start working for Arthur Andersen, at the time one of the largest CPA firms in the world. After two years of squirreling away his net pay, Tom left Andersen to go to NYU law school. He met his wife, Margaret, at a local NYU bar. Margaret was a physical therapist major at NYU who, like Tom, was working her way through college. To help fund her college education, Margaret waitressed at a local pub near NYU. After a number of dates, they fell in love. They married after Tom graduated law school. Tom was able to find a job at a very prestigious law firm in New York City, where he worked for a few years before making the leap to a big company in downtown Manhattan, as part of their company's team of patent attorneys. Not long after, their son Michael was born, followed soon after by Sean and then Matthew. They were living in a townhome in North Jersey for a number of years. Tom worked hard and Margaret was a good saver. After a number of years, they moved next door to me, here in Manasquan. I was outside when they were moving in. I even gave them a hand, as they didn't have a moving company helping them.

"A few weeks after the O'Neills moved in, the Veblens followed. Like Tom O'Neill, John Veblen was a very successful attorney with a wife, Joan, and three young kids. John had worked his way through Albany Law School and, like Tom O'Neill, had gotten a good start working for a prestigious law firm in New York City. He met his wife, there, in fact. She was a legal secretary."

"So, if Mr. O'Neill and Mr. Veblen had such good jobs, how come the Veblens don't live in their home anymore, JC?" Kirsten asked.

JC smiled, winked at Kirsten, and then pulled his cigar out of his mouth, pointing it directly at her. "That, Kirsten, is where my story begins. You see, while my two neighbors may have started out in the same place, they didn't finish in the same place."

JC reached into his beach bag, pulling out a notebook, a mechanical pencil and a ruler, which he then handed to Brendan.

"You're the official scorekeeper, Bren," JC said.

"For what JC?"

"There are a lot of moving parts to this story. Each part is like a piece to a puzzle. We'll cover each topic, one beach at a time. You're going to keep the books, so to speak, for each topic. Now, write at the top of the first sheet the word *Summary Page*. Next, I want you to create four columns. In the first column write the heading *Topic*. In the second column, write down *Tom*. In the third column write down *John*. In the last column write down *John's Difference*."

Brendan did exactly as JC requested and then passed around the notebook so everyone could see.

SUMMARY PAGE

TOPIC	TOM	JOHN	JOHN'S DIFFERENCE

JC turned his head, and stared toward in the direction of his home, ten blocks from the beach. "Tomorrow we head to Sandy Hook, where we begin the story of the O'Neills and the Veblins."

Engagement Stage

S andy Hook is famous the world over. Not only is it the main thoroughfare for the international shipping trade in New York City, but it also gained fame during the Revolutionary War. Sandy Hook was where British war ships often massed along its vast shoreline, preparing for battle in nearby Manhattan or as a staging area for battles fought from Boston to South Carolina.

On the bayside sits the Highlands, a sleepy seaside town, dotted with numerous bars, restaurants, docks, marinas and small homes, all within walking distance to the bay. The bay is fed by the Navesink and Shrewsbury Rivers, which bleeds into the Atlantic Ocean, around Sandy Hook, a barrier island preventing three thousand miles of rolling Atlantic Ocean from breaking at the foot of the Highlands.

Its wide, long, raw beach stretches for seven miles and it was the next stop for JC and his grandkids.

As soon as they were settled in their beach chairs on one of Sandy Hook's many beaches, JC began the next part of his story.

"Tom O'Neill had decided, shortly after starting his new job at the law firm, that he was going to propose to Margaret. Many of his friends recommended he buy the engagement ring at Tiffany's so he could impress Margaret.

The problem was a ring at Tiffany's would set him back at least $5,000 and all he had in the bank was $1,000. Tom didn't want to go into debt in order to buy the ring, so Tiffany's was out. One of his friends knew a jeweler in the Diamond District in New York. If you were good at haggling you could get yourself a great deal near wholesale prices. So Tom, armed with $1,000 in cash and his Socratic haggling skills, left work one night and headed to the Diamond District to make the largest purchase of his life."

JC took a long drag on his cigar. After exhaling, he continued.

"Now, John Veblen, like Tom, had also decided to propose to his girlfriend Joan, shortly after starting his new job at his law firm. John really wanted to impress Joan, so he headed to Tiffany's and found the perfect ring. Unfortunately, the ring cost $5,000 and, like Tom, John only had $1,000. So, John had a decision to make: Should he find a less expensive ring for $1,000 or should he borrow the $4,000 he needed in order to buy the expensive ring from Tiffany's? John decided to buy the engagement ring from Tiffany's and proceeded to visit several banks to see if they would lend him the $4,000 he needed. John spent a great deal of time filling out paperwork for the various bankers. Due in large part to his profession and the prestigious law firm who employed him, one of the bankers agreed to lend John the money. The terms of the loan required him to pay it off over a three-year period at an annual interest rate of eight percent. John signed the loan agreement and received a $4,000 check from the bank, which he immediately deposited into his bank account. A few days later, John marched into Tiffany's with a check for $5,000 and walked out with the engagement ring."

JC pointed his cigar to each of his grandkids. "OK, my little geniuses. Can anyone tell me how much money Tom saved over John?"

Casey's hand shot up immediately. "Four thousand dollars, JC."

"Correct. That's the difference between the cost of both rings. But we're missing something else. Anyone know?"

The eyes of Brendan, Kirsten and Casey darted back and forth between each other, wondering who might have the answer. JC sat back and let their little brains work.

"The loan," Brendan screeched. "John took out a loan and Tom didn't."

"Why is that important?" JC asked.

"Interest," Brendan shot back.

"Right on!" JC exclaimed proudly, pounding both fists on his knees.

"John had to pay the bank interest for lending him the $4,000. Does anyone know how much interest?" JC asked.

Kirsten's arm shot up. "He paid eight percent interest each year for three years. So that's $320 a year multiplied by three, that equals $960." Kirsten beamed a confident smile that let everyone know she nailed it.

"Wow!" JC boomed, praising Kirsten for her quick mathematical mind.

"OK, Bren. In that notebook I gave you on the first line, write the words *Engagement Ring*. That will be our first subject or topic. Now move to the right and under *Tom's* column, write down $1,000. Under *John's* column, write down $5,960. In the last column, the one marked *John's Difference*, write down $4,960."

Brendan did as JC instructed and then handed the notebook to JC to look over.

Engagement Stage

TOPIC	TOM	JOHN	JOHN'S DIFFERENCE
ENGAGEMENT RING	$1,000	$5,960	$4,960

"OK, good. So, as you can see right here," JC was pointing to the $4,960 under the *John's Difference* column, "Tom and John, although in the same profession, making the same amount of money, made two very different decisions about how to spend their money on the engagement ring. John's decision cost him $4,960 more than Tom's. Everyone see that?" JC held up the Summary Page, passing it, left to right for his grandkids to see.

All three nodded in agreement.

"That's all for today. Tomorrow, we head to Sea Bright Beach. The O'Neills and the Veblins will be getting married. So, tomorrow, we all have a wedding to attend."

Wedding Stage

Sea Bright Beach was the next stop along the way for JC and his grandkids. Due to a combination of frequent storms, which batter the New Jersey coastline, and the natural flow of the Gulf Stream, the currents carry sand from South Jersey to Sandy Hook. Sea Bright, unfortunately, was a frequent victim of this shoreline theft. Ironically, this coastline chaos is also what made Sea Bright so unique.

Sea Bright is a half-square mile, narrow barrier peninsula, just south of Sandy Hook. On one side is the Shrewsbury River and on the other side, the Atlantic Ocean. Due to its particular geography, a sea-wall was constructed in an effort to protect the seaside and riverside homes from the onslaught of Mother Nature. These sea-walls, comprised of huge boulders, reinforced by concrete, ran nearly the entire length of Sea Bright, along the beach side, and rose as high as fifteen feet in some places. This one-of-a-kind sea wall makes Sea Bright Beach unique among New Jersey's beaches. And Sea Bright Beach was where JC would share the next part of his story, with his grandkids.

"Weddings can be very expensive," JC said, as they all settled into their beach chairs on the coarse sand that was Sea Bright Beach.

"If you are not careful, those costs can easily get out of control. Where do you have the reception? The nicer the place, the more expensive it will be. How many people do you invite? The more people you invite, the more expensive the reception will be, because most reception halls charge on a per-person basis. Open bar or cash bar? If open bar, how long? Two hours, three hours, four hours? Do you get a limousine? If so, how many limousines? What about the band? Do you get an expensive band or a cheaper band, maybe you get a DJ instead of a band, because DJs are less expensive. How much money do you spend on your wedding dress? How many bridesmaids and groomsmen do you have? Do you pay for the bridesmaids dresses?"

JC paused to let it all sink in for the kids.

"These were the decisions the O'Neills and the Veblins faced. Because they both came from poor families, there was very little either of their parents could contribute to defray the costs. They had to rely solely on their own financial resources. The O'Neills decided the best option was to create a budget and define how much money they were willing to spend. Tom O'Neill figured that if he and his fiancé agreed upon how much they would spend on each wedding decision, that would help remove the emotion from their decisions. The first item on the wedding budget was the reception hall. They set the maximum they would spend at $1,250 for food and $500 for the open bar. They also set the number of guests at 125. So, that meant they needed to find a reception hall that cost no more than $10 per plate, which wasn't easy. After visiting several reception halls, the cheapest one they could find cost $15 per head. They decided to ask family and friends for ideas for a cheaper venue. One of Tom's friends knew of a place called The Monmouth Officer's Club in Monmouth, New Jersey, that charged only $10 a head. They went to visit and found it was your basic reception hall. Nothing fancy. But, at $10 a head, it was far less expensive than other reception halls and within their $1,250 budget. The catch was that you or a family member had to be, or have been, a veteran. Fortunately, both Tom's and Margaret's grandfathers had served in World War I, which qualified them to use the club.

"Their next decision was the open bar. The club charged $3 per head, per hour, for house liquor and a choice of two types of beer and two types of wine, red and white. Tom and Margaret agreed to limit the open bar to two hours, which would set them back $750. Their budget for the open bar was $500, so they would be over budget by $250. The budget for the band was $200. Fortunately, Margaret's childhood neighbor was in a weekend band. They played mostly weddings and similar venues on the weekends, and were happy to play at their wedding for $100, which was a $100 savings. Tom negotiated the flower arrangement by bartering his CPA skills for a year with the florist, so the flowers cost them nothing but Tom's time and expertise, saving them another $100. They continued to go down their list, one after another, making sure they did their best to stay within budget. Limousine? One would suffice at $200. Wedding dress? Margaret settled for an off-the-rack dress that cost $150. It was nothing fancy, but it would do. Tom found a tuxedo in a Goodwill Store and had it custom-tailored, which set him back $75. There were other miscellaneous expenses.

"When all was said and done, the entire wedding cost them $2,625, or $125 over their $2,500 budget. Fortunately, they received gifts totaling $3,625, and this meant they had $1,000 left over after all of their costs. They would use part of that $1,000 to cover their $500 honeymoon, leaving them with an extra $500 to put into their savings account."

JC got up from his beach chair to stretch his legs before continuing his wedding story.

"Come on. Everybody up. Let's stretch a bit to get the blood flowing," JC commanded.

They all stood up, stretching their legs and arms for a few minutes and then they all sat back down to continue the story. "The Veblins made some very different decisions. Unlike the O'Neills, they did not create any budget for the wedding. They did, however, make a list of all of the wedding decisions they had to make. After visiting several reception halls, they settled on one Joan and her mother loved. The only thing was that it was very expensive–$40 a head for the food and the facilities. Forty dollars was very expensive back in 1949. It was the equivalent of, say, $100 in today's 1985 dollars."

"What do you mean, in today's 1985 dollars?" Casey inquired.

JC thought for a moment then blurted out, "Inflation." He then paused, reflecting on how to explain inflation to his grandkids.

"If we were to buy a brand new bike today, how much would we have to pay?" JC asked.

"Sixty dollars." Brendan answered confidently. Everyone nodded in agreement.

"OK," JC responded. "So, the Veblins got married in 1949. Sixty dollars in today's 1985 dollars would only be worth about $25 in 1949 dollars. The reason for the difference is something called inflation. Inflation represents the percentage increase in the value, over time, of anything you spend your money on. Every year, due to inflation, things just get more expensive. For example, if the inflation rate for 1985 was three percent, that means your bike would cost you $62 next year, or 1.03 times more than in 1985. Because of inflation, things get more expensive every year. So, a bike that costs you $60 in 1985 would cost you $62 in 1986, $64 in 1987, $66 in 1988 and so on. So, if you bought a bike in 1949 and it cost you $25, today, in 1985, it would cost you $60. Likewise, the $40 the Veblins paid for each person in 1949, for food and facilities, would cost them $100 today, in 1985."

"Why is that important to the story, JC"? Kirsten asked.

"It's important because the Veblins essentially spent $100 of their future wealth. When you spend money today, what you are really doing is spending your future wealth. Buying a $25 bike in 1949 means you'll have $60 less wealth in 1985. Now, imagine if, instead, you saved that $25 every year for 36 years. That would equal ...," JC did some of his CPA scribbling on Brendan's notepad. "Twenty-five times 36 years equals $900. But because of inflation, that $900 in 1985 would be worth $1,326 dollars today, in 1985, if inflation was 3% every year for 36 years.

The point is that every dollar you spend today dramatically reduces how much wealth you have in the future."

JC paused for a moment, making sure it sank in for his grandkids, then continued his story.

"So, as I said, the Veblins picked a reception hall that would cost them $40 a head. Next up was who to invite to the wedding. They struggled with the guest list. Initially, they just listed everyone each of them wanted to invite. Their initial list had three hundred and six people on it. Knowing that was too many people, they began reducing the number down. Eventually, after much back and forth, they settled on two hundred people. At $40 a head, that would be $8,000. Their next item on their list was the wedding gown. Joan found a picture of one in a magazine that she loved. The problem was that it would have to be custom-made. They found a place in New York City that specialized in custom-made wedding gowns. The cost would be $300.

"Next up, the open bar. The reception hall they selected gave them two options: Basic and Premium. The Basic would cost them $10 a head. This option came with two different types of beer and wine. The Premium would cost $15 a head for top-shelf liquor. It also offered six selections of beer and six of wine. They opted for the Premium package, which would cost them $3,000. One after another, they tackled each item on their list. When they were done, the total cost of their wedding would be $12,000. Even back then, that was a lot of money. Since they had only $6,000 saved for the wedding, that meant they had to rely on wedding gifts to pay the balance. The reception hall agreed to half up front and the remaining half to be paid at the end of the reception. They negotiated similar payment plans with the band, florist, limousine company, etc. The amount of the gifts they received at the wedding totaled $8,000, leaving them with $2,000 for the honeymoon."

JC took the notebook and pencil from Brendan, ripped out a sheet of paper and began scribbling some numbers down on the paper. When he was done, he turned to Brendan. "OK. According to my calculations, all in, Tom spent $2,625 for his wedding and John spent $12,000." Then he handed the notebook and pencil back to Brendan. "Bren, write down the next topic – *Wedding*. Under Tom's column, write $2,625 and under John's write $12,000. That's a difference of $9,375, so put that number under the *John's Difference* column."

Brendan did as JC instructed and showed everyone the updated Summary Page.

SUMMARY PAGE

TOPIC	TOM	JOHN	JOHN'S DIFFERENCE
ENGAGEMENT RING	$1,000	$5,960	$4,960
WEDDING	2,625	12,000	9,375

"Tomorrow, we'll head to Long Branch Beach. We're going on a honeymoon," JC said in his characteristic, booming voice.

Honeymoon Stage

"We're going to spend *two days* here in Long Branch Beach," JC informed his grandkids, as they all settled down in their beach chairs.

"Why two days?" Kirsten asked.

"Well, I was thinking we'd spend one day on the beach and one day on the pier."

"What's on the pier, JC?" Brendan asked.

"Kid's World!" JC screamed, followed by an ear to ear smile.

Casey screamed back, "Kid's World! What's Kid's World?"

"Kid's World is only the coolest place in Long Branch," JC said matter-of-factly.

"Instead of paying for each ride," JC continued, "you pay one price and you get to go on all of the rides as many times as you like. Plus, they have this place called The Haunted Mansion. It's a 10,000 square foot mansion with thirty rooms, secret passage ways and winding tunnels. They have something called The Living Graveyard where the living dead try to reach out and grab you. The actors are made up in all sorts of different scary costumes. Some eat spiders, others want to drink your blood. There are dead people sleeping in open caskets. There are more than thirty creatures of the night." JC was rubbing his hands together, grinning like a mad scientist.

All three of his grandkids returned excited grins.

"But before we go to the pier, I've still got a story to tell. The next part of my story is the O'Neills and the Veblins Honeymoon. Bren, on the Summary Page, write the word *Honeymoon* underneath *Wedding.*" Brendan did as JC requested.

"Being frugal is really nothing but a habit. We can see that Tom appears to have the frugal habit and, so far, John doesn't. But what about their wives? You see, who we pick as our spouse in life can have a profound effect on our financial lives. They can either reinforce good money habits or compound bad money habits. In the next part of the story, you'll see exactly what I mean." JC paused, took a deep breath of the salty sea air and then began his honeymoon story.

"Tom's co-workers suggested that he should take Margaret to Hawaii. Tom was somewhat resistant to the idea because Hawaii was so far away and it was also very expensive. But Tom realized this was not a decision he should make on his own, like he had done with the wedding ring. So, he brought it up to Margaret. Margaret had reservations about a honeymoon in Hawaii, for the same reasons as Tom had. Instead, she suggested that they spend a week down the Jersey Shore. She thought it would not only be less expensive, but it would give them more honeymoon time since they would not have to fly anywhere. In 1949, Ocean Grove was still very inexpensive, as Jersey Shore beach towns go, and it was only ninety minutes from where Tom and Margaret lived in

North Jersey. Ocean Grove had some magnificent historic inns within a block or two of the beach and, so, that's where they decided to go.

"Tom, a former lifeguard who worshipped the beach, absolutely loved the idea of an inexpensive honeymoon at the Jersey Shore. They both did some investigative work and settled on the Manchester Inn, which offered the best value at the lowest price in town. It would cost them $400 for the week. Even better, breakfast and dinner was included in the deal. Margaret figured that even if they passed on a few free dinners, their out-of-pocket bar and restaurant costs would be no more than $100 for the week. So, all in, their honeymoon cost them about $500."

JC stood up. "Come on everyone, up. Let's stretch the old muscles."

Brendan, Kirsten and Casey all hopped to their feet and ran in place for a minute, following JC's lead. Then they all got down on the sand and did ten pushups followed by thirty sit-ups. They were amazed at JC's physique. Even at sixty-nine years of age, he had well-defined muscles covering every inch of his lean runner's body. JC was always exercising and it was on full display, as he guided his grandkids through various exercises. Once they settled back into their beach chairs, JC resumed his honeymoon story.

"OK, so Bren, you know the drill. To the right of the word *Honeymoon*, jot down $500 under *Tom's* column." Bren did as JC requested.

JC leaned forward in his chair. His soft, intelligent eyes locked onto each one of his grandkids, one after the other. "Unlike Tom, John was committed to taking his wife on an exotic honeymoon. He wanted to go to Brisbane, not far from Australia's Gold Coast, a long ways away from New Jersey. Traveling by airplane, in 1949, was still a novelty and very costly. It would be a very expensive honeymoon, he knew and it would mean flying for twenty-six hours each way. Nonetheless, he brought the idea up to Joan. Joan liked the idea, although she wondered if they could afford it. John explained that they had $2,000 left over from the wedding, plus he had a good salary and would be able to make up the difference over time. He just needed to find a travel agent who would allow them to pay over time, whatever the difference was. Joan deferred to John, since he was the one making the money. If he thought they could afford it, then she was all in.

"John suggested that Joan take charge of the arrangements. Joan reached out to a local travel agent in town to help them make the arrangements. The travel agent asked Joan what their budget was. She said they had $2,000 left from the wedding, but that her husband was an attorney in a big law firm in New York City and made a very good salary. The travel agent made some phone calls and in an hour had the all-inclusive honeymooners set up at a cost of $4,000: $3,600 for the trip and $400 for something called a deferred payment fee. Joan didn't know what that meant. The agent said the travel agency charges ten percent of the cost of the trip to clients who cannot pay the entire amount up front. Joan argued that they were paying $2,000 up front and that they should only be charged ten percent of the balance. The agent explained that this wasn't how it worked. Joan went home to discuss this with John. He told her if they wanted to go to Australia, what choice did they have? So, they ended up paying the extra $400."

JC pointed to Brendan who without being told, wrote $4,000 under John's name, then calculated the difference and put it under the *John's Difference* column.

"What have you got?"

"Thirty-five hundred dollars," Brendan replied, as he showed everyone the updated Summary Page.

Summary Page

TOPIC	TOM	JOHN	JOHN'S DIFFERENCE
ENGAGEMENT RING	$1,000	$5,960	$4,960
WEDDING	2,625	12,000	9,375
HONEYMOON	500	4000	3,500

"Brilliant!" JC bellowed, flashing a huge grin. The following day, JC was true to his word and took his grandkids to the Long Branch Pier, Kid's World, where they spent the day on rides, eating cotton candy, and getting the hell scared out of them at The Haunted Mansion.

First Apartment Stage

The excitement of Long Branch still dripped over Brendan, Kirsten and Casey as they disembarked from the RV at Asbury Park.

"Do they have rides here too, JC?" Casey asked hopefully.

Unfortunately, the once great and historic Asbury Park had fallen on hard times and in 1985 it looked old and neglected. A former bastion of the well-to-do from New York City and North Jersey in the 1920s, 1930s and the 1940s, it was now, sadly, in disrepair. The opening of the Garden State Parkway, Monmouth Mall and Great Adventure, forced the relocation of many merchants, along with their attorneys and accountants. Riots broke out in the 1970s that resulted in much destruction. JC wanted to take his grandkids to the Palace Amusements before it closed its doors at the end of the summer. Plus, Asbury Park still had a big, beautiful boardwalk along the perimeter of its wide beach.

"This place used to be a major casino back in the day," JC said, as they made their way along the beach, searching for just the right spot. "Second only to Atlantic City. Tens of thousands came here every summer to vacation and have fun. There was nothing quite like it on the Jersey Shore. Unfortunately, it's a shadow of its former self. One day, I hope, they will revive Asbury Park, because it is really a beautiful beach," JC said in a somewhat somber tone.

Once they were all situated in their beach chairs, JC resumed his story of the O'Neills and the Veblins.

"When most couples start out in life, they typically rent an inexpensive apartment, until they can save enough money to start a family and buy a home. The O'Neills and the Veblins were no different. Because Tom O'Neill worked in New York City, he and Margaret wanted to find an inexpensive apartment that was close to New York. They visited many towns in northern New Jersey and finally settled on an apartment in Hoboken that fit their budget. Many Irish-Americans lived in Hoboken in 1949 and Tom, having grown up on Staten Island in a big Irish community, wanted something familiar. Also, the Port Authority had recently completed the Holland Tunnel, which made Tom's commute from Hoboken to New York a short one. The monthly rent would be $150 and the commuting costs into New York would be about $20 a month. So, all in, Hoboken would cost them $170 a month."

JC lit up a fat Churchill cigar, before continuing.

"John Veblin wanted to be able to walk to work, so he and Joan focused on finding an apartment in mid-town Manhattan. Although they would save money on commuting, rent in that area was fairly expensive. They eventually settled on a very small studio apartment that would cost them $300 a month. The O'Neills and the Veblins both remained in their apartments until 1955."

JC squinted, eyeing each one of his grandkids. "OK, how much did they spend during those six years?" JC asked.

Silence followed by more silence. JC, patiently waited and waited. Finally, Brendan's hand shot up. "The O'Neills spent $12,240 and the Veblins spent $21,600. That's a difference of $9,360." JC asked for the notebook and began scribbling some numbers on it. "Right you are Bren. Now add a new topic called *Apartment Rental*, right under *Honeymoon* and log it on the Summary Page."

Brendan had already done that while JC was scribbling his numbers and immediately showed everyone the updated Summary Page.

Summary Page

Topic	Tom	John	John's Difference
Engagement Ring	$1,000	$5,960	$4,960
Wedding	2,615	12,000	9,375
Honeymoon	500	4000	3,500
Apartment Rental	12,240	21,600	9,360

Saving For First Home Stage

"We don't have very far to drive," JC said as they all sat down for breakfast at the small kitchen table inside JC's RV. As usual, JC had been up several hours before his grandkids. Waiting for them were JC's famous home fries, bacon, sausage, pancakes, toast and perfectly cooked scrambled eggs. JC loved cooking breakfast for them. His eyes glimmered with happiness as he sat watching them eat.

"How far is it to Ocean Grove from Asbury Park, JC?" Brendan asked.

"We could literally walk to Ocean Grove from here," JC said. "It's that close. But then we'd have to lug all of the chairs, the umbrella and our cooler along the boardwalk. The boardwalk is connected from Asbury Park to Ocean Grove to Avon to Belmar, and finally to Spring Lake. So we could actually walk along the boardwalk, all the way to Spring Lake if we wanted to," JC said.

"How long is that?" Kirsten wondered.

"It's about seven miles," JC responded.

"I can do it," Casey boasted.

"You wouldn't make it to Avon," Brendan teased her.

"Would too," Casey countered.

"Would not," Brendan said.

This went on for a few seconds before JC interrupted their back-and-forth bickering. "Does anyone know why Ocean Grove is different from every other beach town in New Jersey?"

Blank stares from his grandkids, was all JC received in response. After a few seconds, JC broke the silence. "It's the only town where people don't actually own the land their homes sit on," JC said.

"Who owns the land JC?" Kirsten asked.

"It's owned by a religious organization called the Camp Meeting Association. I think their religion is called Methodist. The Association owns everything, even the beach. Everyone who buys a home in Ocean Grove enters into a renewable ninety-nine-year lease with the Association. You can even pass down your home on to your children if you wanted to. The Association controls everything. It's a good thing it's Tuesday and not Sunday," JC commented.

"Why's that?" Kirsten asked.

"The Association keeps the beach closed on Sunday until 12pm," JC responded.

"And you'll notice there are no bars in Ocean Grove," JC continued.

"They're a dry town. Can't sell alcohol in Ocean Grove. But they have a beautiful beach, just waiting for us outside these doors." JC motioned to the RV doors, and they exited the RV, filled the beach wagon, and headed to the beach.

Once they were all settled in the beach chairs, JC pointed at Brendan. "Now, where were we? Bren, where did we finish up yesterday?"

"*Apartment Rental,*" Brendan responded, after looking over his Summary Page.

"Well, I think we should talk about the savings habits of the O'Neills and the Veblins," JC suggested.

JC asked Brendan to add another topic under *Apartment Rental* called *Savings*. Brendan did as instructed and JC began the next part of his story.

"The O'Neills were very good savers. During their six years renting in Hoboken, they were able to save $300 a month. It wasn't easy, but they had a plan. Tom got paid twice a month from his law firm. He'd give the check to Margaret, who would deposit it the next day at the bank. After a few days, when the check cleared, she would go back to the bank and write out a check to Cash in the amount of $200. She would then deposit $150 into a savings account the O'Neills had set up. The other $50, she and Tom split. Tom would get $20 to use for his commuting and other expenses, and Margaret would keep $30 to buy groceries, clothing and other things for the house. Tom brought his lunch to work nearly every day, which reduced their expenses and Margaret would shop around for discounts on clothing and other small things they needed for the home. She even clipped coupons to keep the grocery bills down. The rest of the money in the checking account went to pay the rent, utilities, insurance, and other living expenses. If they had extra money left in the checking account at the end of the month, Margaret would write out a check to Cash and deposit that extra money into the savings account."

"Didn't they have any fun, JC? Sounds like they never spent any money to go out to restaurants or the movies or do any fun stuff," Casey said.

"Oh they had fun. They'd do all of those things. They'd go out on Fridays and Saturdays with certain friends, the ones who were frugal like them. You see…." JC paused for a moment to gather his thoughts and then continued.

"It's very important to surround yourself with the right people in life. People who are like-minded. In the O'Neills case, the friends they associated with the most were all very careful with their money. They all had a frugal mindset, so this made it a lot easier for the O'Neills to stick to their savings strategy. If their friends were spenders and not savers, it would have been hard for the O'Neills to stick to their savings strategy."

"Why's that?" Casey asked.

"Habits are contagious," JC said. "They spread like a virus within your social circle. If you hang around spenders, you'll become a spender. If you hang around frugal people, you'll become frugal. The O'Neills realized this out early on, so they made a point of hanging out with people who shared their frugal mindsets. You ever notice that people who drink a lot, tend to hang out with other people who drink a lot? People who go to the track to bet on horses, tend to hang out with people who go to the track to bet on horses also. It's just human nature. We like to herd with the same flock. If you want to adopt a good habit, just hang out with people who have the habit you want to adopt. That's kind of what the O'Neills did. And that's why they were able to save so much money." JC paused for a moment before continuing.

"Who wants to see if they can beat me in a race?" JC had his mad scientist grin going. He reached into his bag and pulled out three pencils and then handed them out to each of his grandkids.

"Bren, give us all a piece of paper from your notebook." Brendan ripped out three pages and gave one to Kirsten, Casey and JC.

"OK. Now let's see who can be the first one to figure out how much money the O'Neills saved during their six years living in the apartment? Ready, set, go!"

The grandkids frantically began to scribble numbers on their individual piece of paper. JC pretended to do the same. Kirsten's hand was the first to shoot up in the air.

"Got it. $21,600," she proclaimed confidently.

JC pretended to do some more scribbling, as if to verify Kirsten's answer.

"Right you are my little angel. Right you are." JC praised Kirsten, who gushed with pride.

"I'm guessing, that…" JC stopped mid-sentence and began scribbling something on his paper. When he was done scribbling, he resumed talking.

"I'm guessing that, in today's dollars, that $21,600 would be worth about $72,000."

"Wow. That's a lot of money," Brendan howled.

"It certainly is," JC responded. "Unfortunately, the Veblins were not very good savers. During their entire time in their New York apartment, they were only able to save $5,000. And, when I get into the next part of the story, when they buy their first home, you'll see how important that savings amount becomes. Let's update that Summary Page, Bren."

Brendan did just that and showed the results to everyone.

SUMMARY PAGE

TOPIC	TOM	JOHN	JOHN'S DIFFERENCE
ENGAGEMENT RING	$1,000	$5,960	$4,960
WEDDING	2,625	12,000	9,375
HONEYMOON	500	4000	3,500
APARTMENT RENTAL	12,240	21,600	9,360
SAVINGS	21,600	5,000	16,600

"Time for ice cream," JC announced.

Ocean Grove was a quaint town, dotted with dozens of shops: ice cream stores, shoe stores, clothing stores, cafes and stores that sold all sorts of beach supplies and equipment. They even had a small theatre where they showed movies and put on plays. The town was right out of a Norman Rockwell painting.

They found the perfect, quaint ice cream parlor and sat outside. When they all had finished eating their ice cream, they headed back to the beach, just a few short blocks away.

Home Purchase Stage

JC shifted his chair away from the creeping Ocean Grove sunlight that had begun to fry his feet. Once JC was completely shaded by the big umbrella, he moved on to the next part of his story.

"Thanks to their frugal money habits, Tom and Margaret were able to save $21,600 while living in their apartment. They decided to put $10,000 of their savings down on a townhouse, which cost them $30,000. They were ready to start a family and figured a townhouse would provide them with the space they needed to start their family. Buying a home, at this time, made sense to the O'Neills. They figured that by owning a home they could build up some equity every time they made a mortgage payment. Plus, if the value of the townhouse went up, that would increase their equity even more. Buying a home meant they had to get a mortgage from the bank for $20,000. Because they were putting so much down on the home, they were able to find many banks willing to lend them the money they needed, and at interest rates as low as three per-cent. The bank they decided on gave them the option of paying them back in fifteen years, rather than thirty years. This way, they could pay off the loan quicker and build equity quicker."

Casey interrupted JC. "What's equity?"

JC paused and considered the question for a moment. "Equity is like a savings account," JC replied. Casey still seemed confused, so JC tried a different angle.

"Every time you make a payment to the bank on a loan they give you to buy a home, you reduce how much money you owe the bank. That means you own more of your home. That's equity. One day you're going to sell that home. You're hoping that when you do, you get more money than you originally paid for the home. That increase in the value of the home is equity too. The more equity you have, the more money you'll have when you sell your home. You can then use that extra money to buy another home. Understand?" Casey nodded her head and JC continued.

"Now, shortly after the O'Neills purchased their townhouse, they decided it was a good time to start a family. They were shooting for three kids. They knew that eventually they would have to move out of the townhouse and into a bigger home, as the townhouse would be too small for five people. Having thought this through, the O'Neills decided that it would be smart to pay more to the bank than they were required to pay each month on the loan. They agreed to pay an extra $200 a month on the mortgage. That extra $200 a month increased their equity in their home by $200 every month. They figured that when they sold their home, all of those extra payments would add up and increase their equity even more.

"They remained in their first home for five years. When they sold their townhouse, they had built up so much equity that they were not only able to buy a home close to Manasquan Beach, they were also able to do so with a very small mortgage. A smaller mortgage meant lower monthly loan payments to the bank, which also meant less interest they had to pay to the bank. When they sold their townhouse, they settled on a $50,000 sales price. Because they were paying an extra $200 a month on the mortgage, when they sold their townhouse, they only owed the bank $4,000."

JC pointed his cigar at his three grandkids. "OK. Can anyone tell me how much equity the O'Neills had when they sold their home?" Kirsten shot her hand up first. "$46,000."

"Correct!" JC clapped his hands, leaned over and gave Kirsten a big kiss on the forehead.

"But, there's one thing I forgot to tell you. When they eventually sold their home for $50,000, they had to pay something called closing costs. Closing costs are fees you have to pay to different people who help you when you sell your home. Real estate agents, attorneys, title companies and a few others all get some money when you sell a home. Real estate agents get the most, typically five percent of the sales price of the home, when they help you sell a home. When the O'Neills sold their home, they decided to do it on their own. So, Margaret put an ad in several newspapers and eventually sold it to the highest bidder. This saved them how much?" JC asked. Brendan blurted out, "Twenty-five hundred dollars."

"Correct!" JC said, slapping Bren on the side of his right shoulder. Brendan beamed back a proud smile.

"They had to give some people involved in the sale $1,000. So, now, how much equity did they have left over after paying all of their closing costs?" JC asked his grandkids.

There was silence for a few seconds, then Casey shot up to her feet and screamed "Forty-five thousand dollars!"

"Right you are, my little Cassedia," JC chuckled. "Let's do the math so everyone agrees: $50,000 less the mortgage balance of $4,000, less closing costs of $1,000 equals $45,000. Everyone got it?" All three shook their heads in agreement and JC continued his story.

"Because John spent a lot of money on the wedding ring and because he and Joan wiped out their savings in order to go on their honeymoon, they didn't have much in savings when it came time for them to buy their first home. So, they had to settle for a $25,000 condominium. Condominiums don't increase in value like townhouses or regular homes do. Plus, they didn't have much in savings to put down on the home. During their five years living in the apartment in New York City, they were only able to save $5,000. They wanted to use only $3,000 of that for the down payment so they could use the remaining $2,000 to buy furniture and fixtures for the home. Because they only had $3,000 to put down, they struggled to find a bank who was willing to lend them the money they needed, which was $22,000. And because the down payment was so low, the bank required that they pay an interest rate of five percent over thirty years. This meant they would have to pay much more in interest than the O'Neills had to pay, plus it would take them much longer to pay off the mortgage."

"And less equity in their home. Right JC?" Casey interrupted.

"That's right Cassedia," JC responded.

"As it turned out, just like the O'Neills, the Veblins would sell their first home five years later and buy their Manasquan home. When they sold their condominium, they still owed $20,000 on the mortgage. Using a real estate agent, they found a buyer who was willing to pay $30,000, which was only $5,000 more than what they had paid for it. The agent's fee was $1,500 and the other closing costs added up to $1,000. Anyone know what their equity was when the sold their home?" JC was greeted with blank stares.

"Let's do the math," JC said. "Thirty thousand dollars, less $20,000, less $1,500, less $1,000 equals $7,500."

JC eyed his grandkids, making sure they were all on the same page.

"OK, Bren. Now, let's record the O'Neills $45,000 in equity and the Veblins $7,500."

Brendan followed JC's instructions, added the topic *Home Equity* and, without instruction, calculated the difference, put it under the *John's Difference* column and showed his calculation to JC and the girls.

Summary Page

Topic	Tom	John	John's Difference
Engagement Ring	$1,000	$5,960	$4,960
Wedding	2,625	12,000	9,375
Honeymoon	500	4000	3,500
Apartment Rental	12,240	21,600	9,360
Savings	21,600	5,000	16,600
Home Equity	45,000	7,500	37,500

JC nodded his approval. "That was a lot of money back then," he said.

After everyone scanned the updated Summary Page, JC continued with his story. "The low down payment negatively affected how much equity they could build up in their Manasquan home, because they would be paying less every month in principle on the mortgage. Even worse, because they couldn't put at least twenty percent down on their home, they had to pay an extra $50 a month for something called PMI. PMI is insurance required by the bank for borrowers who put down less than twenty percent. This meant a higher monthly mortgage payment than Tom and Margaret had to contend with. That higher mortgage meant they had less left over at the end of the month to put into their savings. All of these things, the higher mortgage, PMI, decreased savings, and lower home appreciation on the condominium, had a negative compounding effect on their finances and limited how much they would be able to save in the future."

JC got up out of his chair and declared it was body surfing time. Brendan, Kirsten and Casey launched themselves out of their chairs and raced JC to the water.

Growing Family Stage

" **J**C, you said the Veblens money decisions had a domino effect on their finances," Kirsten said with a confused look.

"That's right," JC replied.

"But their Manasquan home is way bigger and way nicer than the O'Neills home?" Kirsten countered.

"And bigger than yours, JC," Casey added.

Kirsten and Casey were struggling with this one. The Veblen's Manasquan home was much bigger and nicer than the O'Neills home and even JC's home.

"That's true," JC said. "Their home is much bigger and nicer than our homes. I'm gonna cover that in the next two parts of our story. Just bear with me," JC smiled and continued his story.

"All of the financial decisions Tom and Margaret made with the wedding ring, the honeymoon, the purchase of their townhouse and paying down their mortgage paid big dividends when they decided to buy their Manasquan home. As we saw, when the O'Neills sold their townhouse they had accumulated a significant amount of home equity, and that extra home equity came in handy when they purchased their Manasquan home.

"Because of all of that home equity they had built up, the O'Neills were able to put much more money down on their Manasquan home than the Veblen's could afford to do. In fact, because they were such good savers, they were able to put down $60,000 towards the purchase of their $100,000 Manasquan home. That meant they only had to ask the bank for $40,000 in order to finance the purchase of their new home. Because they were putting so much money down, and because they were able to pay off the mortgage over fifteen years, the bank was willing to lend them the $40,000 at a very low interest rate of just 2.5 percent. That lower monthly mortgage payment meant they had more money left at the end of the month. The O'Neills decided to pay an additional $300 a month to help them pay off their mortgage sooner and they put another $300 into their savings."

JC got up from his beach chair, clapped his hands and motioned to the lunch cooler.

"Lunch time," he proclaimed. "Let's get some grub. After that, we'll take a walk on the boardwalk. Then we'll get back to the story. Sound like a plan?"

Everyone nodded, and JC began dishing out the food and drinks. When they were done with lunch, they headed toward the boardwalk.

An hour of fun and games flew by before they decided to head back to their beach chairs. Once they got settled in, JC resumed his story. "Where were we?" Brendan handed JC the notebook. JC eyed it over carefully.

"Ah yes, the Veblins Manasquan mortgage. Although the Veblen's were purchasing the same $100,000 home as the O'Neills, from the same home builder, the Veblins opted for certain upgrades that cost them $10,000 more. Builders are always trying to sucker new home buyers into spending more money on upgrades. It's almost always a bad deal. Upgrades are where home builders make the most profit. They know that new home buyers are very excited and often get caught up in the moment, with emotions running high. The builders' pitch is that the upgrades will only cost them a few more dollars every month, which they would hardly notice. Smart home buyers suppress the emotional impulse to upgrade.

"The Veblins, unfortunately, were unable to control their emotions, like the O'Neills were able to, and agreed to the $10,000 in upgrades. When they went to the banks to get a loan for their home, they informed the banks that they could only put down ten percent. This meant they needed to shop around for bank who would be willing to lend them $99,000. Eventually, they found a bank who would do this, but the bank required them to pay 5.5 percent in interest because a lower down payment represented more risk to the bank. That higher mortgage translated into a higher monthly mortgage payment, which meant they had very little left over at the end of the month to put into savings."

JC pointed his cigar at Brendan. "Now Bren, on the Summary Page, write down *Manasquan Mortgage* below *First Home*. Under *Tom's* column write down $40,000. Under *John's* column, write down $99,000. Now, subtract the two and in the *John's Difference* column write down $59,000."

Brendan did as JC instructed, then passed around the Summary Page to the group for inspection.

Summary Page

Topic	Tom	John	John's Difference
ENGAGEMENT RING	$1,000	$5,960	$4,960
WEDDING	2,625	12,000	9,375
HONEYMOON	500	4000	3,500
APARTMENT RENTAL	12,240	21,600	9,360
SAVINGS	21,600	5,000	16,600
HOME EQUITY	45,000	7,500	37,500
MANASQUAN MORTGAGE	40,000	99,000	59,000

"As we can all see from the Summary Page, all of the financial decisions the Veblins had made started to add up. They spent $4,960 more for the engagement ring, $3,500 more for their honeymoon, had $37,500 less in home equity on their first home, and their mortgage on their Manasquan home was $59,000 more than the O'Neills. You may think that bad money habits aren't a big deal on the small stuff, but when we make big financial decisions, like buying a home, those bad money habits have a significant effect. When we have bad financial habits, we often don't realize how those bad habits cause ripples, affecting everything else we do in life. In the Veblins case, their bad money habits forced them to get a much higher $99,000 mortgage, which was $59,000 more than the O'Neills. And for thirty years they were going to have to pay for those bad money habits."

JC asked Brendan for the notebook and on a separate page JC used some of his CPA skills to calculate how much interest the O'Neills and the Veblins would have to pay over the life of their loans.

"One hundred and three thousand dollars is what the Veblins will have to pay to the bank over thirty years. The O'Neills only have to pay back $8,000, or $95,000 less in interest."

"That's a lot of money," Kirsten said.

"Darn right, Kirsten," JC responded.

"That's money that could have gone into their savings account," JC continued.

"Bren, we better add another category under *Manasquan Mortgage* and call it *Mortgage Interest*," JC suggested.

Brendan made the change to the Summary Page and this is what it now looked like:

SUMMARY PAGE

TOPIC	TOM	JOHN	JOHN'S DIFFERENCE
ENGAGEMENT RING	$1,000	$5,960	$4,960
WEDDING	2,625	12,000	9,375
HONEYMOON	500	4000	3,500
APARTMENT RENTAL	12,240	21,600	9,360
SAVINGS	21,600	5,000	16,600
HOME EQUITY	45,000	7,500	37,500
MANASQUAN MORTGAGE	40,000	99,000	59,000
MORTGAGE INTEREST	8,000	103,000	95,000

Home Improvements Stage

" We're headed to the Irish Riviera," JC said as he turned the key to the ignition on his RV.

"Why do they call it the Irish Riviera?" Casey asked

"Oil tycoon Martin Maloney would take his family to Spring Lake in the early 1900s. Soon other well-to-do Irish families, who knew Maloney, began summering in Spring Lake too. Eventually, it became a summer destination for many rich, Irish families and now it holds the distinction of having the largest population of Irish Americans of any town in New Jersey. But more than that, what makes Spring Lake so unique is the magnificent Victorian homes with their wrap-around porches."

"Can we walk around the town and look at the homes, JC?" Casey asked.

"We will do just that, as soon as we find a parking spot for the RV," JC said.

As promised, JC and his grandkids took a two-hour stroll around Spring Lake. After the tour, they stocked JC's beach wagon and headed for the beach, where JC resumed his story.

"The O'Neills did very little in the way of home improvements to their house. They spent $4,000 expanding the front porch, wrapping it around the entire house. A few years later, like me, they finished off the basement and added two small bedrooms and a full bath. They even used the same contractor as I did. The total cost, like mine, was about $2,500. Other than those improvements, like me, they just maintained their home."

JC asked Brendan to add the $6,500 for the *Home Improvements* topic to *Tom's* column on the Summary Page.

"The Veblins house is like twice the size of your house and the O'Neills house, JC," Brendan commented, as he penciled in the $6,500.

"It's actually more than twice the size. If you include the finished basement, the O'Neills and I have about 3,100 square feet of space in our homes. The Veblins have close to 6,500 square feet of space. They transformed their home into the biggest and most expensive house on the block, and the second most expensive home in Manasquan. It was a mini-mansion. I think there are ten bedrooms in that house. The average home in Manasquan has three bedrooms, so it really stood out, which, I guess, is what they were looking to do. They wanted to impress people with their home while they lived in it. And they suc-ceeded. People who didn't know them as well as I did just assumed they were multi-millionaires. They spent more than $6,000 in finishing off their basement.

"A few years after they finished off the basement, they made a huge addition to their home, which doubled the size of their home. The contractor had talked the Veblins into including a basement under the expansion. I tried to talk John out of it, since he had already finished off his original basement, but he didn't listen. That meant all of the money they spent on the original finished basement was wasted because the contractors pretty much undid all of the work that was previously done on the basement. It took about a year and $30,000 before they were done with the addition. They then had to furnish all of that extra space, which cost them $4,000. Then, not two years later, they decided to add a pool, which set them back another $6,500. Then they had to buy all new outdoor pool furniture, which was another $2,500 and then they built this huge, stone deck in the back-yard that butted up against the pool. That was another $4,500."

"Where did they get the money for all of those improvements, JC?" Casey asked.

"They literally spent everything John made," JC replied. "Plus they refinanced their home, adding another $30,000 in debt, so they could afford to do the addition. And, worse, their new, higher thirty-year mortgage meant they were starting from scratch in paying off all of that mortgage debt."

Brendan didn't wait for JC. He immediately totaled up all of the additional home improvement costs. "That's $53,500. Jeez. That's a lot of money," Brendan said, as he added the new topic, *Home Improvements*, logged the additional costs onto the Summary Page and then showed everyone the results.

Summary Page

Topic	Tom	John	John's Difference
Engagement Ring	$1,000	$5,960	$4,960
Wedding	2,625	12,000	9,375
Honeymoon	500	4000	3,500
Apartment Rental	12,240	21,600	9,360
Savings	21,600	5,000	16,600
Home Equity	45,000	7,500	37,500
Manasquan Mortgage	40,000	99,000	59,000
Mortgage Interest	8,000	103,000	95,000
Home Improvements	6,500	53,500	47,000

"What were they thinking, JC?" Brendan asked.

"They weren't. John, like Tom O'Neill, was a very good attorney. And every year John would get a good raise, along with a bonus. He just felt his income was going to keep going up and up. And it did. But, unfortunately, so too did their spending. It's called lifestyle creep. They spent John's increased income as fast as he made it," JC said.

"Lifestyle creep?" Kirsten responded with a crooked face.

JC thought for a moment how he would explain lifestyle creep to a thirteen-year-old.

"Lifestyle creep is when you increase your standard of living in order to match your increased income. It's one of those Poor Habits I talk about all the time in my books and my seminars."

JC asked if Kirsten understood but before Kirsten could respond, Casey jumped in. "What does standard of living mean?"

JC considered Casey's question for a few moments, then responded. "Every household has a standard of living. A standard of living is basically how much money you have to spend every month in order to live as you do. People accumulate a lot of stuff in life – homes, cars, clothing, bikes, etc. The more stuff you accumulate, the more expensive your standard of living becomes. It also includes everyday things we need or want–food, clothing, shoes, haircuts, medicine, school supplies, vacations, etc. The two things that force your standard of living costs to go up the most are your home and your cars. The more expensive your home, the higher your standard of living costs will be. You have to pay real estate taxes to the town you live in. You have to repair your home when something breaks. You have to pay utility bills, like gas and electric, so you can have heat in the winter or air conditioning in the summer. The bigger your home, the more it costs to heat it and to keep it cool.

"Those with a high standard of living generally have more expensive homes than other people. They might also have more expensive cars. They might go on more exotic vacations than everyone else. A high standard of living means your costs to live the life you want to live are high. A low standard of living means your costs to live the life you want are low. When the Veblins decided to make all of those expensive improvements to their home, they dramatically increased their standard of living costs. As John's income increased, he and Joan used that additional income to finance their super-sized life." JC inched his body closer to his grandkids. "We'll see, later on, how their home improvement decisions would come back to haunt them as their kids were about to enter their college years. Now Bren, I want you to add up the difference column, so we can all see the enormous effect of the O'Neills smart money habits compared to the Veblins poor money habits."

Brendan did some math. After a few moments he held up the Updated Summary Page for all to see.

Summary Page

TOPIC	TOM	JOHN	JOHN'S DIFFERENCE
ENGAGEMENT RING	$1,000	$5,960	$4,960
WEDDING	2,625	12,000	9,375
HONEYMOON	500	4000	3,500
APARTMENT RENTAL	12,240	21,600	9,360
SAVINGS	21,600	5,000	16,600
HOME EQUITY	45,000	7,500	37,500
MANASQUAN MORTGAGE	40,000	99,000	59,000
MORTGAGE INTEREST	8,000	103,000	95,000
HOME IMPROVEMENTS	6,500	53,500	47,000
SUBTOTAL			$282,295

JC whistled loudly.

"JC, why didn't you use your Rich Habits to help stop them from doing more damage to themselves?" Casey wondered.

JC smiled a crooked, knowing smile at Casey, then he reached into his bag and pulled out a cigar, clipped and lit it. He knew this was going to be an important conversation.

"No one wants to talk about money. It's such an emotional, personal, touchy subject. That's one of the reasons why so many struggle with money. No one talks enough about what to do and what not to do. Most people, including parents, prefer to bury their heads in the sand, like Ostriches, and ignore talking about money with their children. If no one shows you how to manage your money, how are you supposed to know what to do?" JC asked rhetorically, before continuing.

"When I started making my home improvements, Tom and John both came over to my house to find out what I was doing. We all sat in the backyard. I pulled out a few cigars and a couple of beers. I showed them the blueprints for my home improvements, as we smoked our cigars and drank our beer. I went over all of the costs. Tom liked what he heard and asked if he could borrow my blueprints when I was done so he could duplicate what I was doing. 'Why reinvent the wheel?' Tom said. That made me feel good. John then told us he and his wife were thinking about making some improvements to their home as well. I offered him my plans, as well, but he said he and his wife had something different in mind. He wanted to finish off his basement. He also wanted to add a big addition and a pool. I told him that that would cost a lot of money.

I told him those improvements would make his home one of the biggest, most expensive homes in Manasquan. I informed him that expensive homes don't sell very well in Manasquan. John didn't seem to care. He had recently bought a very expensive boat and it bothered me that they were spending their money as fast as John made it.

"So, one day I saw John and his wife sitting in their backyard and got the courage up to have a conversation with them about money. They knew all about my Rich Habits books and they knew I travelled the world teaching people about my Rich Habits. I did my best to try to explain to them my Rich Habits smart money philosophy. But it went in and out their ears. I really tried. But, I failed. I just knew they were digging themselves a hole they would never be able to climb out of. Over the course of the rest of their lives, you'll see how the Veblins poor money habits ultimately put them in the poor house."

The Savings Mindset

Their routine was to drive to a new beach every morning. JC's grandkids typically slept through the short commute, while JC drove. Once JC arrived at their new beach destination, he would put on his running sneakers and head out for a three-to-four mile run every morning. Most beaches had outside showers and when JC finished his run, he'd find one and shower off. The kids would start to wake up when JC began rattling around his pans to start breakfast. They'd eat their breakfast in the RV, take showers outside, get into their bathing suits, load the beach wagon and everyone would head off to the beach.

The next beach on their journey was Point Pleasant Beach. Point Pleasant was famous for their boardwalk. Jenkinson's Amusement Park was located right on the boardwalk. Thousands visited it every day. It had so many rides – roller coasters, two rock climbing walls, a Merry-Go-Round, rides that spun you in all directions, and a pirate's ship that swung back and forth, like a pendulum. They also had five blocks of arcade games. There was even an aquarium on the boardwalk. JC told them they would spend two days at Point Pleasant; one day on the rides and the next day on the beach. When they stepped onto the boardwalk, Brendan, Kirsten and Casey's eyes lit up like roman candles. Kirsten and Casey were holding hands, jumping up and down in excitement. JC let them loose. They bolted like cannon balls out of a cannon.

"Stay together," he yelled, as he jogged slowly behind, trying to keep up. "Damn, I wish I had their energy," he said to himself.

JC followed them from ride to ride. He even went on a few rides with them, like the roller coaster. JC loved roller coasters even more than his grandkids did. They spent most of the day at Jenkinson's. It was a long day and everyone was exhausted when dinner time rolled around. It would be an early night, JC thought to himself, as they ate dinner. And he was right. Brendan, Kirsten and Casey all fell asleep half way through a movie they were watching inside the RV. While they slept, JC unlatched the bunk beds from the sides of the RV, set up the pillows and the blankets and then, one by one, helped each child up and onto their respective bed. JC, exhausted himself, hardly got through two pages in a book he was reading during the trip, before falling fast asleep.

Everyone overslept. JC, who normally woke at five am every day, didn't open his eyes until he heard the seven am beach tractors begin their early morning beach raking, preparing the beach for another day of beach lovers. JC marveled at the machine-like automation involved in readying the beach. New Jersey's beaches were truly a huge, money-making enterprise. Every day, thousands of visitors and vacationers descended upon each beach, spending their hard-earned dollars for a little slice of heaven. By mid-afternoon, the beach would be a sea of umbrellas of all shapes, sizes, and colors—candy to the eyes of the beach lover.

Despite their late start, there was plenty of beach left at nine am. Most of the crowd would not arrive until ten am. As usual, they found a great spot, close to the water. You had to know the tides really well before you set up your spot. Depending on the moon, low tide usually lasted until noon. Then the ocean began its slow march forward. If you didn't plan right, you'd lose your spot to the sea and have to search around for another. The smart ones, like JC, always set up their umbrellas and chairs about fifty feet from the receding waves at low tide. This way, when high tide rolled in, they wouldn't have to move an inch. Plus, at high tide, they would be that much closer to the water.

"Proper preparation prevents poor performance," JC bellowed, after spotting the ideal spot for them on the beach.

"High tide's a little earlier today," JC added, as he marked his spot.

"It's already begun moving in, so we need to be about thirty feet from the water, I figure." JC then began marking off the distance. Like a soldier marching in formation, JC counted as he marched. "Twenty-eight, twenty-nine, thirty." JC stopped and surveyed the beach, their spot, and the shoreline and then planted his umbrella.

"Right here. Here's our spot." JC's face exploded with a big smile, confident he had, once again, conquered the ocean and its diabolical high tide plans of disruption.

JC drove the umbrella forcefully into the sand. JC was strong. Even at sixty-nine, he had bulging biceps, powerful shoulders, a fully developed six-pack abs and the pecs of a bodybuilder. It wasn't genetics. One of JC's Rich Habits was daily exercise. Every day, JC ran three to five miles. Every other day he lifted weights. The only thing that looked sixty nine on JC was his grey hair. Every other part of his body looked like it was forged in steel.

"Bren. Where did we leave off?" Brendan took a look at his Summary Page.

"We finished with *Home Improvement*, JC," Brendan replied.

"Ok. Perfect. The next topic I'd like to cover in my story is the savings mindset. There are four ways to build wealth. You can save and invest your savings. You can become a senior executive at a big company. You can become a virtuoso, or top expert in whatever it is you do for a living. Or, you can become an entrepreneur by pursuing some dream. The O'Neills chose the Saver-Investor path. It's really the guaranteed way to build wealth. This path has only two rules you need to follow. The first rule is to save twenty percent or more of your income by living off of eighty percent or less of your income. When you follow the first rule, you must adjust your lifestyle and keep your living costs down in order to be able to live off of that remaining eighty percent."

"The second rule is to consistently and prudently invest your savings. Those who save twenty percent or more of their income, starting at an early age, and then prudently invest their savings, will be able to sock away a lot of money over time. Some are even able to retire in their mid-forties. That's what the O'Neills did, they pursued the Saver-Investor Path. They had the savers mindset. In fact, they saved much more than twenty percent. They saved close to forty percent of their income. It was truly a team effort. Tom and Margaret, early into their marriage, set a goal of saving forty percent of every paycheck, which forced them to live off the remaining sixty percent. This strategy helped them to automate the savings process. I kind of touched on this when we were talking about the O'Neills first apartment. Margaret would deposit Tom's check. After the paycheck cleared, she would write out a check equal to forty percent of Tom's net pay and deposit it into a savings account.

"When they accumulated enough money in the savings account, Tom and Margaret would consult with their financial advisor, who would help them research certain stocks or mutual funds. That research would take a few months for the O'Neills. When they were finished doing their investment homework, they would call their financial advisor, instructing him what to buy. Tom and Margaret prudently invested by only buying stocks or mutual funds they had done their homework on. They would also automatically reinvest the dividends they earned from the stocks/mutual funds to buy more. That's known as dividend reinvestment. They followed this savings-investment process for most of their adult lives. Eventually, their stock and mutual funds portfolio grew very large.

"In the late 1970s, they also started to diversify their savings by investing in real estate. Because Manasquan was a very popular summer vacation spot, people would pay good money to rent a home for a week for their family. Tom and Margaret knew Manasquan very well and decided to start buying homes so that they could rent them out to families during the summer. Since Tom made a good salary and they had great credit, significant savings and a large stock portfolio, the banks were happy to lend them money at a low interest rate. The O'Neills would typically put down about twenty-five percent and finance the rest of the home by getting a loan from the bank. They would never buy a home unless the rents they received exceeded the costs associated with owning the home. Those costs included the mortgage, which was always a fifteen-year mortgage for the O'Neills. The costs also included real estate taxes, utilities, repairs and maintenance, etc.

"During the late 1970s and early 1980s, they bought six rental homes this way. Their goal was to pay off the mortgage on each rental home in ten years by paying more than the bank required. And this is precisely what they did. It was a good plan, but it required some sacrifices. They didn't go on any fancy vacations. They would use one of their rental homes for a week, usually before and after the summer rental season, as their vacation. They held on to their cars for at least ten years. They mowed their own lawns and maintained the rental properties themselves. They bought second-hand, high quality clothes from the Goodwill stores and then had them tailored so they would fit. By the time the O'Neills were in their mid-forties, they were multi-millionaires. But you'd never know it. Their house was average. Their cars were old. Their clothes were not fancy. Margaret didn't have much jewelry to speak of. Theirs was a very ordinary, lower middle-class lifestyle."

JC reached into his beach bag and pulled out a Montecristo cigar. His favorite was the Churchill-styled cigars. He used to jokingly say, "Besides beer, women, gambling and drugs, it's my only Poor Habit." The truth is, it was JC's *only* Poor Habit. When he discovered the Rich Habits so many years ago, he had worked very hard reinventing himself by changing his habits. But his cigar smoking was one Poor Habit, he decided long ago, he would never surrender.

After JC clipped and lit his cigar, he resumed his story. "The Veblins were not savers. They didn't have the savings mindset. They spent every dollar they earned. They invested much of their excess earnings in their home. They also liked to go on fancy vacations. Their kids had been to Disney World numerous times. They went on cruises with their kids. They rented expensive homes on the beach. Joan had the finest jewelry. John had a fetish for expensive watches. Hard to believe, but he actually had three Rolex watches. Every three years they bought a new car. They threw expensive parties at their opulent home. They went to restaurants several times a week. Then there was the boat obsession that John got into in the late 1970s. He spent a lot of money on different boats. Those boats had to be docked, which cost money and they had to be repaired, which cost money.

"Despite my best efforts to get the Veblins to change their money habits, they never did. Saving money was, unfortunately, an afterthought for the Veblins. He eventually would become a partner in his law firm, which only gave them more money to spend. They never forged that important savings Rich Habit. Their Poor Habit of constantly supersizing their life, whenever John made more money, would bite them in the butt later on. We'll get into that on another beach."

Child Education Stage

As JC started the RV's engine, he turned his head to the back towards his grandkids, "If you thought the Point Pleasant boardwalk was cool, wait till you see Seaside," he said in a tone that stirred their imaginations. During the ten-minute commute to Seaside, JC regaled them on the sights, sounds, and attractions that soon awaited them in Seaside.

"Seaside has one of the widest beaches of all of the beaches on our journey. It even has an amusement park. If you thought Jenkinson's was big, wait till you see Seaside's amusement park. It's twice the size. It has a four story Ferris wheel. They have a big roller coaster that goes a hundred feet in the air. Every year they add new rides. Not sure what they added this year, but we'll find out soon enough. Next to Great Adventure Amusement Park in Jackson, New Jersey, it's the largest amusement park in the Northeast."

"We're going to need three days for Seaside," JC roared.

"Three days!" Casey and Kirsten screamed in tandem.

"Three days. Can't cover Seaside in just two days," JC said.

"And I have another surprise. We're going to spend a night in one of Seaside's best motels, right on the beach. It's got a big pool with a ten-foot diving board and a water slide. And every room in the motel surrounds the pool. You can literally walk out of your room and right into the pool. We're even going to go crabbing. Ever been crabbing before?"

"Never," Brendan said. "I always wanted to, though."

"What's crabbing?" Casey asked.

"Catching crabs," JC responded matter of factly. "We're going to go out in the early morning, when the tide is low, and throw some metal crab traps into the ocean off the dock. If the crabs are biting, we'll catch a bunch of crabs. Then, we're going to eat them."

"Eewh," Casey cried. "We're gonna eat crabs?"

"Yep. I'm going to throw them in a big pot, boil them up, crack them open, and put a bunch in my amazing, home-made spaghetti sauce for us to eat with dinner. I'll leave a few crabs and show you how to pound their shells and pull the crab meat out of their claws. Then we're going to take a boat cruise and watch the sun set on the boat. We'll spend the last day on the beach."

JC had his grandkids in a fever of excitement. He just loved riling them up.

JC delivered on every one of his promises. It was an exhilarating and exhausting two days for everyone. On their final day, they headed for the beach. Once they were all settled in their beach chairs, JC looked over at Brendan. "OK, Bren. Where'd we finish off?"

Brendan opened up the notebook. "The last topic was *Home Improvement*," Brendan said.

"Good. OK. Next topic we'll call *Child Education*," JC responded.

Brendan immediately went to the Summary Page of his notebook and wrote down the next topic – *Child Education.*

"Tom and Margaret were raised on Staten Island, which is a suburb of New York City. They had both attended public schools there. Staten Island had a pretty good public school system at the time. When they were looking for a place to raise their family, they decided on Manasquan because Tom and Margaret loved the Jersey Shore, and Manasquan had a pretty good public school system back in the 1970s and the 1980s. They wanted to raise their kids in a beach town that had a good school system and Manasquan fit the bill very nicely. In New Jersey, we pay a lot more in real estate taxes than other states because New Jersey's real estate taxes directly fund the public school system. In other states, they fund the school system with income taxes, sales taxes, hotel taxes, and all sorts of other taxes. New Jersey does it this way so that the local school district can control the schools, rather than the politicians in the state government. That's one of the main reasons why New Jersey consistently has the best performing public schools in the nation. But, these great schools come at a cost. New Jersey has, by far, the highest real estate taxes in the country which, unfortunately, makes New Jersey an expensive place to raise a family." JC pulled a water out of the cooler before continuing.

"Now the Veblins did things a little differently. They decided to send their kids to private school. John's wife, Joan, believed private schools provided a superior education than public schools. You see, Joan was raised in the Bronx, which is a suburb of New York City. The public school she attended was not a very good one and, as a result, Joan had developed a bias against public schools. I know she and her husband, John, had fought over this. John was raised on Staten Island, which had a pretty good public school system. They just were not on the same page when it came to schools. Joan won that battle, but it came at a price. They sent their kids to some very expensive private schools that set them back about $1,000 per child, per year. Since they had three kids, it was quite an expensive investment in their education. I estimated that they spent about $30,000 for private schools over the years. That's about $80,000 in today's dollar, just to give you some perspective."

Brendan looked up at JC, wondering if he was done with that part of his story. He wasn't exactly sure what to log onto his Summary Page. JC saw the confused look on his face.

"You only need to mark down the $30,000 in John's column, show the difference, and then add that to the $282,295 *Subtotal*. Both were paying real estate taxes, so we'll consider the real estate taxes they paid a wash for this topic." Brendan did as JC instructed, then showed everyone the updated Summary Page. JC let out another loud whistle when he saw the grand total in the *John's Difference* column.

Child Education Stage

Summary Page

TOPIC	TOM	JOHN	JOHN'S DIFFERENCE
ENGAGEMENT RING	$1,000	$5,960	$4,960
WEDDING	2,625	12,000	9,375
HONEYMOON	500	4000	3,500
APARTMENT RENTAL	12,240	21,600	9,360
SAVINGS	21,600	5,000	16,600
HOME EQUITY	45,000	7,500	37,500
MANASQUAN MORTGAGE	40,000	99,000	59,000
MORTGAGE INTEREST	8,000	103,000	95,000
HOME IMPROVEMENTS	6,500	53,500	47,000
SUBTOTAL			$282,295
CHILD EDUCATION	0	30,000	30,000
			$312,295

87

Career Management Stage

" I used to take your dad and your aunts to Long Beach Island every summer, before we moved to Manasquan," JC said. "In fact, at one time I considered moving our family to Beach Haven in LBI. That's what we called it – LBI, for short. But, I decided the Manasquan public school system was better and plus, at the time, I was traveling a lot to New York, doing speaking engagements on my Rich Habits research. LBI was just too far away from New York and Manasquan had a train that went directly into New York Penn Station. Anyway, we'd spend two weeks in Beach Haven, usually in July. Your dad and your aunts loved it. A lot of memories there," JC said as he navigated his RV off exit 63 on the Garden State Parkway.

"Eight more miles," JC said, as he turned the wheel on his RV towards the inter-coastal bridge that would take them to LBI.

"Besides Sea Bright, this is the only beach that doesn't have a boardwalk. Instead of a boardwalk, the entire town is like one big amusement park. They have something they call Bay Village. In Bay Village, they have Fantasy Island Amusement Park. At Fantasy Island there are all sorts of rides and an entire building filled with nothing but arcades and electronic games. When we're done with Fantasy Island, we'll walk next door to the water park. The water park has one of the longest water slides in the world. There are actually four of them, so you can all race each other. They also have Cowabunga Beach at the water park, where you have to climb and navigate all sorts of obstacles. Lastly, they have the Lazy Crazy River, where you can just float around in tubes – that's the lazy part. Then there's the crazy part where you get bombarded with a big water-filled bucket that tips over. Next door to the water park, they have a huge miniature golf course." JC paused, letting it all sink in, before continuing.

"Like Point Pleasant, we'll need to spend two days in Beach Haven. One day at Bay Village and the second day on the beach. Sound like a plan?" JC asked.

"Sounds like the best plan I've ever heard of," Kirsten almost screamed.

"You're amazing, JC," Brendan said.

"Best Grandpa in the world," Casey added.

Learning and fun go together so well, JC thought to himself, as he crossed the inter-coastal bridge and onto the island he fondly called LBI.

Bay Village was a big hit. For eight hours they rode roller coasters, raced down water slides, floated in the lazy river, and played miniature golf. The whole day seemed to go by in a flash to everyone, especially JC. When they were done, they walked across the street from the rides to Bucalews, where they had dinner, talked about their amazing day and made plans for the following day.

"Tomorrow, we head to the beach. It's probably the smallest beach on our trip. But if we get there early, we can find a great spot." JC continued, "Let's find an ice cream parlor and finish off our day in style."

His grandkids smiled, tired smiles. JC knew they would not last long, so they found an ice cream parlor close to their RV to close out the day.

Early the next morning, the four lugged their beach wagon, chairs, cooler, and supplies to the beach. After JC consulted with the newspaper on the tides, he did his ritualistic marching to find the perfect spot on the beach. When he was done, they set up the umbrella and settled into their beach chairs to listen to the next installment in JC's story of the O'Neills and the Veblins.

"Both Tom and John were fine attorneys who were well-liked and well-respected at their respective law firms. But the grueling hours were too often pulling them away from their families. Because Tom and Margaret had done such a good job saving and investing their money, Tom was able to take a slightly lower-paying job, working as a patent attorney for a large, publicly-held pharmaceutical company in Princeton, New Jersey. While the new job did not pay as much as he was making at the law firm, it did offer the potential for significantly more compensation in the form of stock grants and stock options. Tom and Margaret figured if the company did well, that stock compensation could one day be significant, as the company's stock value increased. A major factor in their decision was the reduced commute. Tom's new job reduced his daily commute from four hours to less than ninety minutes. The new job also demanded fewer hours. His fifty-hour work-weeks at the law firm became forty-hour work-weeks with his new employer.

"With the shortened commute and the less demanding hours, this meant Tom had more morning and evening time for Margaret and the kids. Tom relished the idea of seeing his kids off to school in the mornings and having dinner with the family at night. Something that was previously a rare luxury now became a daily ritual for Tom. Plus, now Tom had more time to exercise every day. Margaret used to refer to Tom as a weekend warrior because Tom would try to squeeze as much exercise into his weekends as he could. With this new job, Tom was able to exercise every morning before work. He'd jog three miles each morning, followed by two hundred pushups, two hundred sit-ups and some stretching. Tom's exercise routine improved his health dramatically. He lost twenty-five pounds, his blood pressure went down, and he felt more energetic. Thanks to their disciplined saving, financial thrift, and modest living standards, this career change was a dream come true for the O'Neills."

JC reached for his water, took a sip, and then resumed his story. "John Veblin, on the other hand, continued to work long hours for many years at his law firm. He would typically leave for work six am every morning and come home at nine pm every night, except Fridays, when most at the firm called it a day at four pm. Every Friday and Saturday night, John and Joan would join a group of their closest friends and dine at a fancy restaurant. John rationalized this expensive Friday ritual as something he earned after a long week of work. That left Saturdays, Sundays, holidays and vacation days for the kids, who grew accustomed to John's absence. Eventually, John would make partner, which came with a significant increase in pay, but the hours remained unchanged.

"Because of his grueling work schedule, John had no time to exercise. His weight ballooned, he developed high blood pressure and his blood sugar levels became elevated. As a result, John had to take medicine every day in order to manage his poor health. But, John had no choice but to continue logging in long work days. They had little in savings and investments. John needed the law firm as much as it needed him. Eventually, when he retired, the pension from the law firm would provide he and his wife with all the income they would need. At least that was the plan."

Life's Unexpected Consequences

"When people think of Atlantic City, they think casinos," JC said, as he navigated his RV onto the Garden State Parkway, en route to Atlantic City, their next destination.

"In the 70s they legalized gambling in Atlantic City. Within a few years they started building one casino after another: Resorts, Regency, Bally's, Caesar's, the Sands, Harrah's, the Golden Nugget, the Playboy Hotel, the Tropicana and two Trump casinos. People flocked from not only New Jersey but from Connecticut, New York, Pennsylvania, Maryland, Delaware and other states. Gambling is a Poor Habit. I like to think of it as a poverty tax; a tax on poor people. Atlantic City was built on that gambling Poor Habit. What a shame," JC said, shaking his head from side to side.

"Why are we going to Atlantic City then JC?" Casey asked.

"Well, Atlantic City also happens to have one of the widest beaches and longest boardwalks of all of the beaches in New Jersey. The boardwalk goes on for four miles. It's known as the grandfather of boardwalks. Twenty-six million people visit Atlantic City every year, not only to gamble but also to visit its white, sandy beach. Plus, there are a lot of restaurants and amusements, and arcades. We'll spend the morning on the beach and then take a walk on the boardwalk, so you can see what it's all about. Then we'll have dinner at one of the oldest and best restaurants in Atlantic City called the Knife and Fork Inn."

The commute from Long Beach Island to Atlantic City took only twenty minutes. JC was able to find a spot for his RV, only a few blocks from the beach. Immediately, they began loading the beach wagon and headed to the beach.

"I remember it like it was yesterday," JC said, beginning the next installment of his story about the O'Neills and the Veblins.

"I was working on one of my books in my home office late one Saturday morning when I heard an awful scream coming from the Veblins back yard. It was Joan Veblin. I ran down the stairs of my office, jumped over the fence that separated our yards from one another, and ran over to Joan, who was bent down over John. John was unconscious on the ground. Joan was desperately trying to give him mouth-to-mouth resuscitation, but was doing it all wrong. I literally pulled Joan off John, told her to call an ambulance and, for the longest three minutes of my life, I gave John CPR. Thankfully, he came around and regained consciousness. He was confused and so scared. I talked calmly to him until the ambulance and their emergency medical service people arrived. They were able to stabilize John in the ambulance as they frantically drove to the hospital. John had suffered a major stroke in addition to a serious heart attack. He spent over two months in a rehabilitation facility. The doctors told John he would never fully regain his speech or the use of the left side of his body. John was just fifty years old, with one kid in college and two more right behind. And he was now permanently disabled. He would not be able to work another day in his life."

JC's grandkids looked around at each other. Shock etched hard on their faces. "What happened to them, JC?" Casey, asked, almost in tears.

"Well, the Veblins had very little in the way of savings. John received a small payout from the law firm for his interest in the partnership. The firm also provided John with a small pension, but it was not enough for them to live on in their Manasquan home. They certainly couldn't afford to continue paying for college for their oldest, who had just begun his sophomore year at Notre Dame University. Joan pleaded with the school for some financial assistance. She filled out all sorts of paperwork. The school turned them down, however, telling them their assets were too high. The value of their home, the home they had invested so much money in over the years, disqualified them from receiving any financial aid. When their son finished his fall semester, he was forced to return home and sit out his spring semester until they could figure things out. Joan then reached out to me for guidance. I went over all of their bills and told Joan the only viable option was to sell their home. They would need every penny from the sale of their Manasquan home to live on for the rest of their lives, I told her.

"Because the real estate taxes in New Jersey were so high, I told Joan they would either have to find something affordable in New Jersey to rent or move out of the state so they could buy an affordable home that did not have such high real estate taxes. College, I told her, was no longer an expense they could afford. After this very difficult conversation, I took down the name of their banker, the one that held the mortgage to their home. I paid him a visit. At the banker's office, their banker said if the Veblins were to sell their home they would probably get about $350,000 at the most, minus selling expenses. All of the other homes in Manasquan were selling for far less, the banker told me. Many were selling for less than $150,000. It would be difficult to find someone who would pay so much money for their home when so many other homes were selling for much less. Plus, I found out they owed $250,000 on the mortgage. That would leave them with less than $100,000 to live off of. That, I knew, wasn't enough.

"I went back to Joan and gave her the bad news. I told her I would cover their son's college costs at Notre Dame and pay all of their housing costs until they sold their home. It took two years to sell that home. The only buyer interested agreed to pay only $275,000, which meant they had virtually nothing left over from the sale. I ended up purchasing a townhouse in Pennsylvania for them to live in for the rest of their lives. I paid for college for their two girls, when they reached college age. It was a difficult time for the Veblins and their kids. But in the end, the kids were ok, which was all I really cared about."

JC turned his head and stared at the waves in the distance, breaking at the foot of the shore. He was lost in thought. Brendan, Kirsten, and Casey stared at JC in quiet admiration.

College and Retirement Stages

"**N**ext to Long Beach Island, I think Cape May is my favorite beach town," JC commented as they made their way along the boardwalk of the last beach along their journey.

"Every time I visit Cape May I wonder why I never moved here. It's bigger than most beach towns, yet still has the small beach town feel. You know, very quaint, homey kind of feel,"

Once they got settled in their beach chairs, JC continued. "No more beaches after this," JC said. This will be our final destination on our journey, sorry to say. It was a fun trip, wasn't it?" JC smiled at his grandkids.

"I'll never forget this trip, JC," Brendan said.

"Me either," Kirsten chimed in.

"I don't want it to end," Casey said with a pout..

"All good things must come to an end," JC said, mimicking Casey's pout.

"But it ain't over yet. I still have a story to finish," he added.

"Unlike the Veblins, the O'Neills had planned very carefully in funding college for their three kids. They not only set aside savings for college, they invested those savings wisely, with the help of their financial advisor. Plus, they had six summer rentals in Manasquan that had gone up in value significantly over the years. And if need be, they figured they could sell one of the rentals to help get their kids through college, but they never did have to sell any rentals. Their oldest boy, Michael, went to Dartmouth. Sean, a few years younger, followed Michael to Dartmouth. Their youngest, Matthew, attended Providence College. Tom and Margaret were so grateful that they could afford to send their kids to such prestigious schools and give them great head starts in life. Your dad and Michael are still the best of friends. And your Aunt Kellie actually dated Matthew O'Neill for a few years after college, while she was in med school. I thought they might eventually get married, but fate had other ideas. Matthew's job took him to Tokyo and they drifted apart. Anyway, shortly after the kids left the roost, Tom O'Neill's company was bought out by a rival pharmaceutical company. The buyout freed up the restricted stock Tom owned and…"

"What's restricted stock?" Brendan said, interrupting JC in mid-sentence.

JC thought a moment. "Sometimes publicly held companies give stock to their senior executives and restrict or forbid them from selling the stock for a number of years. Tom owned about a million dollars of this restricted stock. The terms of the buyout allowed Tom to sell his restricted stock, but only if he accepted an early retirement package. Tom took the package. He already owned $500,000 in non-restricted stock, so this meant he now owned $1.5 million in stock he could sell at any time. They had about $2 million in other stock investments, plus their six rental properties. So, Tom retired a multi-millionaire in his early fifties. Like me, they still spend most of their time in Manasquan. And, like me, they own a second home in

Pensacola, Florida, just a few blocks down the street from my house. Tom always took my advice, unlike John Veblin. John never took my advice, unfortunately."

JC Jobs Smart Money Principles

That night, after Brendan, Kirsten and Casey had fallen asleep, JC reached into the storage compartment under the front console of his RV. Inside were three binders, with each binder brandishing the name of each of his grandkids. This would be JC's parting gift; something to remember the trip by.

Morning arrived. While his grandkids slept, JC griddled some pancakes, fried some bacon, eggs and his famous home-fried potatoes. His grandkids awoke to a kitchen table lovingly adorned with placemats, tableware, orange juice, milk, and a basket of freshly baked muffins from a local bakery.

"Our last meal," Casey said, somberly.

"Our last meal," JC responded, sadly.

They ate slowly, as if by dragging out the meal they could extend the trip indefinitely. When they finished eating, JC gathered up all the plates, glasses and tableware, placing them in the RV's small dishwasher. JC then sat down at the front of the kitchen table, looking at each one of his grandkids and holding three binders between his hands.

"It will take us about two hours to get to Manasquan," JC said. "Your parents will be waiting for us. I told you the story about the O'Neills and the Veblins for a very good reason. There are powerful lessons to be learned from the way each lived their lives. I want to make sure those lessons, and the memory of our adventure, stays with you forever."

JC than handed each one of his grandkids his/her own personalized binder.

"Inside each binder are all of the lessons I want you to take away from our story. Within the pages of each binder is all you need to know in order to live a successful, amazing, happy life. That binder will be the most important thing you will ever own. Keep it near and keep it safe. Not only will it remind you of our amazing journey, it will help guide you through every stage of your life."

JC stood up, headed to the front of the RV, turned the key, and started the engine.

Brendan, Kirsten, and Casey opened their binders and began reading.

JC's Smart Money Principles

Smart Money Principle #1 – Good Habits Good Life – Bad Habits Bad Life

The O'Neills had good habits. Their good habits were responsible for creating the amazing life they lived. The Veblins had bad habits. Their bad habits dragged them down, ultimately destroying their lives.

Habits have a purpose. They save the brain from work and help conserve brain fuel. Habits allow each of us to perform tasks without thinking. Habits are really four things: habitual behaviors, thinking, emotions and decision-making. Your daily habits, as boring as they may seem, are the secret to success, failure or mediocrity. Your behaviors, decision-making, emotional responses and your thoughts can create a life of abundance or a life of scarcity. There are two types of habits:

1. Ordinary Habits
2. Keystone Habits

Ordinary habits are simple, basic, standalone habits – taking a daily shower, the route you take to work, how you hold a fork, etc.

Keystone habits, on the other hand, are very powerful habits that cause a ripple effect on your life. Keystone habits do two things. First, they foster the creation of complimentary or supportive habits, and, secondarily they melt away opposing habits – habits that interfere with the keystone habits.

For example, a young woman named Carrie read my book *Rich Habits*. She was inspired by the book and wrote me a letter. In the letter, Carrie confessed she weighed two hundred pounds. She was officially obese and felt very depressed. Carrie said she wanted to quit smoking and get healthy. She saw my book in a bookstore and bought it. She was excited about changing her habits and asked me what I would recommend. I wrote Carrie back and told her to start walking one mile a day for seven days in a row. I told her to just focus on that first week. I then told her that if she completed that first week of walking, I wanted her to then increase her walking by a mile every week for another three weeks. After those four weeks passed, I told her to begin jogging one mile a week for thirty days in a row, then increase her jogging by a mile every month for the next three months. I also asked Carrie to send me updates on her progress. Well, Carrie wrote me about a year later to tell me about her progress.

After completing the four months of jogging, she said she had lost twenty-five pounds. She felt so good about her jogging, she continued jogging almost every day for several months and lost another twenty pounds. Carrie felt confident enough to enter a local 10K race. In preparation for race, she decided to cut back on how much she was eating, in the hope she would lose more weight before the race. Carrie also cut back on her cigarette smoking from a pack a day to a few cigarettes a day. By race time, Carrie had lost another ten pounds. When she finished the race, she said she felt so very proud of herself. She also felt a surge of confidence. This boost in confidence motivated Carrie to enter a half marathon. In order to prepare for the half, Carrie decided to stop smoking altogether. By race time, Carrie had lost another fifteen pounds and people began calling her skinny. She was elated and on cloud nine from all of the compliments.

Aerobic exercise is a keystone habit. When I asked Carrie to start walking and jogging, I knew that the aerobic exercise would give birth to other complementary habits, like eating healthier. I also knew that if the keystone habit stuck, Carrie would eventually give up smoking. One keystone habit, exercise, literally transformed Carrie in less than a year. That's the power of keystone habits.

Every habit results in an outcome. Some habits cause happiness, sadness, financial success, poverty, good health, bad health, short or long lifespans. There are also habits that increase your IQ, such as reading to learn every day, daily aerobic exercise and pursuing dreams/goals. There are habits which improve relationships, such as the hello call, happy birthday call and life event call. There are habits that improve job performance, such as deliberate and analytical practice and daily study. Below are some of the major habit categories.

Happiness Habits

You know happiness when you feel it. By definition, happiness is the sustained absence of negative emotions and an ongoing presence of positive emotions. Neurotransmitters are chemicals released when one or more neurons (brain cells) communicates with other neurons. Dopamine is the neurotransmitter for happiness. It is one of sixty neurotransmitters produced by the brain. When neurons release dopamine, it creates a sensation that we call happiness. When our dopamine level drops below its baseline, it creates a sensation we call sadness. If dopamine levels stay below that baseline for more than a few days, we call that depression. Depression is devastating to your health and causes a reduction in energy, which impairs productivity and creativity. When we are depressed, we pull back and retreat from life. We become listless and lose all interest. Almost all activities cease and we isolate ourselves from others. It is a widespread, common affliction that affects hundreds of millions of people each year. It's critical, therefore, to develop habits that maintain or elevate your dopamine baseline in order to prevent sadness and depression from wreaking havoc in your life.

What are the Happiness Habits?

- Daily Exercise—Human beings are genetically hardwired for motion. Exercise sets in motion a domino effect of chemical reactions within the body. I'll get into the importance of exercise in more detail shortly, under the Health Habits topic.
- Daily Learning—Humans are genetically hardwired to learn. The brain likes novelty. Our inborn natural curiosity is why we are explorers and inventors. Your brain likes it when it's put to use learning new things. When you learn something new, your brain releases BDNF, a nerve growth factor that is like miracle grow for brain cells, along with the

neurotransmitters dopamine and serotonin. These happiness chemicals are your brain's reward for helping it grow brain cells. Reading every day to learn is one of the most powerful happiness activities you can engage in.

- Growing Constructive Relationships–Human interaction is critical to happiness. More importantly, being in good company, surrounding yourself with other upbeat, optimistic people, elevates your dopamine and oxytocin (another powerful happiness neurotransmitter) levels. Being alone or associating with negative types of people, reduces the production of dopamine and oxytocin. Worse, these relationships create stress. If that stress lasts more than a few hours, it can lead to chronic stress. Chronic stress weakens your immune system. A depressed immune system reduces your resistance to colds and infections, causes plaque to build up in your arteries, which leads to heart disease and also turns on various genes that can lead to cancer. Making a habit out of associating with other happy people helps keep chronic stress away and will help keep you happy and healthy.
- Practiced Positivity–Many studies have shown that making a habit of being upbeat, positive and optimistic makes you happier and more successful in school, sporting activities, and in your business or careers. Meditation, inspirational reading, positive affirmations, and expressing gratitude every day for what you have all boost positivity, which lifts your dopamine levels.

Savings Habits

Develop a Savings Mindset Early in Life
Self-made millionaires who build their wealth through saving, start saving at an early age. The more you are able to save at an early age, the more wealth you'll accumulate. If you want to be financially independent during retirement, save and prudently invest twenty percent or more of your income.

Establish Savings Goals
Self-made millionaires establish savings goals. They save money in order to buy a home. They save money in order to fund college educations for their kids. They save money to fund their retirement. They save money so they can invest that money and build their wealth.

Automate the Savings Process
Self-made millionaires automate the savings process. This is where the rubber meets the road – implementation. They create a system that works best for them and they stick to it for many years. When you automate the savings process, you put wealth accumulation on auto-pilot.

Health Habits

Maintaining your health is critical to living a long, healthy, positive and energetic life. Here's a list of the healthy habits that will get you there:

Daily Exercise

Exercise triggers the release of hormones known as endorphins and also triggers the release of dopamine and serotonin, two powerful neurotransmitters. These chemicals all work in tandem in changing your mood and emotions from negative to positive. If you exercise daily, it is harder for depression to take root. Daily exercise also reduces stress.

Healthy Eating

Making a daily habit of eating more nutritious food and consuming less junk food and alcohol, improves your well-being, provides adequate protein to the body, keeps your good and bad cholesterol in balance, reduces your blood sugar level, and prevents obesity. Healthy eating also reduces your appetite by feeding the bacteria in your gut with the fiber they need to survive and thrive. Eating right and reducing the number of calories you consume to less than two thousand calories a day, helps maintain your health by reducing the accumulation of fat. Fat stores toxins in your body. Less fat, therefore, means less toxins. You want to make a habit of eating more fish, more vegetables, more salads, and healthy meats such as chicken and turkey. Avoid unhealthy meats such beef, ham, bacon, hot dogs and sausage. Unhealthy meats impair your cardiovascular system, elevate bad cholesterol, increases the accumulation of fat and are high in calories. Also, while more expensive, organic food does not have any pesticides. Pesticides can accumulate in the body and lead to a higher risk of cancer.

Habits That Grow Your Brain and IQ

We now know that the brain changes every day. We can rewire our brains (called neuroplasticity) throughout our entire lives and even well into our eighties. We also now know that the hippocampus gives birth to thousands of new neurons every day (called neurogenesis). Thanks to the study of the genome, we've learned that it is possible to increase your IQ over your lifetime. IQs are not fixed. Just because you were a "C" student at age seventeen with an IQ of onehundred, doesn't necessarily mean you will stay that way. You can increase your IQ all during your life with a few habits that have the effect of turning good genes on and bad genes off.

Self-made millionaires do certain things every day that continuously improve their brains and increase their intelligence during their lifetimes. These activities increase brain mass by increasing and strengthening old neural connections and by creating entirely new neural connections.

Daily Learning

Every time you learn something new, you re-wire your brain. New neurons are recruited and begin firing with one another. This is known as a synapse. As new neural pathways are created by learning, your brain actually increases in size and your intelligence grows. Eighty-eight percent of the wealthy in my Rich Habits Study, long before they struck it rich, formed the daily habit of engaging in thirty minutes or more of self-education reading. This single, simple daily habit, alone, helped them to increase their cognitive abilities, which contributed to their success much later in life.

Daily Aerobic Exercise

Aerobic exercise floods the bloodstream with oxygen. This oxygen eventually makes its way to the brain. Oxygen does two things: #1 – It is a catalyst used to convert glucose or ketones into ATP, the ultimate fuel source for every cell in the body. #2–It is a free radical sponge. Oxygen flows around inside each cell, soaking up free-roaming electrons. The oxygen then passes through the cell membrane, with electrons in tow, and flows into the bloodstream. That blood eventually makes its way to the lungs and the oxygen is converted into carbon dioxide, which is released into the air with every breath you take. The more we exercise, the more oxygen we take in and the more free radicals are soaked up by this oxygen-sponge process.

Aerobic exercise also reduces the incidence of obesity, heart disease, high blood pressure, type 2 diabetes, stroke and certain types of cancer. Twenty to thirty minutes of aerobic exercise every day has been proven to stimulate the growth of axons and axon branches on each brain cell. Recent neurological studies have found a correlation between the number of axons and axon branches inside your brain and intelligence. More axons and axon branches translates into higher intelligence. Aerobic exercise also increases the release of neurotrophins, or Nerve Growth Factor (NFG). NFG stimulates the growth of brain cells, helps maintain a healthy coating around every axon of every brain cell (called the myelin sheath), and improves synaptic communication between brain cells. Increased synaptic communication translates into better memory and faster recall. So, daily aerobic exercise feeds the brain, cleans the brain and increases your intelligence, each and every time you engage in it.

Aerobic exercise also boosts your high-density lipoprotein, also known as good cholesterol, and lowers your low-density lipoprotein, also known as bad cholesterol. The result? Less buildup of plaque in your arteries. Studies show that people who participate in regular aerobic exercise live longer than those who don't exercise regularly. Healthier people have fewer sick days and more energy, which translates into more productivity at work. More productivity makes you more valuable to your organization, customers or clients, which translates into more money. Long-term stress impairs our immune system's ability to fight off viruses, diseases, germs and parasites. Because aerobic exercise floods the body with oxygen, this increased oxygen reduces the effects of stress on the body. Aerobic exercise is like a double in baseball; it reduces the effects of stress while at the same time reducing stress itself.

Drink in Moderation
Our livers are able to process about two ounces of alcohol an hour (about two twelve ounce glasses of beer an hour). Anything in excess of that allows alcohol to enter your bloodstream which is then carried to your brain. Once alcohol reaches the brain, it infiltrates the glutamate receptors in your synapses, damaging the neurons' ability to fire off signals. If you regularly drink in excess, you are causing long-term damage to these receptors and this

can cause permanent damage to your memory and your motor skills. Is it a coincidence that eighty-four percent of the wealthy in my study drank less than two ounces of alcohol a day? I don't think so.

Get 7- 8 Hours Sleep Each Night

Everyone who sleeps goes through four to six sleep cycles a night. Each cycle lasts about ninety minutes. Each of these sleep cycles is composed of five separate levels of sleep: Alpha, theta, delta, rapid eye movement (REM) and then back to theta. For each individual sleep cycle, the first three sleep levels (alpha, theta and delta) lasts sixty-five minutes. REM lasts twenty minutes and the final level of sleep, theta, lasts five minutes. The number of hours you sleep is less important than the number of complete sleep cycles you have each night. Five complete sleep cycles a night is considered optimal. Completing less than four sleep cycles a night, however, negatively affects your health. REM sleep is particularly important, as its primary function appears to be long-term memory storage. During REM sleep, what you learned during the day is transported to the hippocampus, which acts as a sort of temporary storage waiting room. If you do not complete at least four, ninety-minute sleep cycles a night, long-term memory storage becomes impaired. Completing at least four sleep cycles, the night after learning new information or a new skill, locks in the new information or new skill. If you get less than four complete ninety-minute sleep cycles the night after learning anything, it's as if the learning never occurred. Sleep helps you remember what you learned during the day.

Experiment with New Activities

Every time you engage in a new activity and then practice it, you grow your brain. When you regularly repeat new activities, the brain cells communicating with each other begin to form a permanent neural pathway, thus growing the size of your brain. It is critical for older people to engage in new activities in order to keep their brains active and prevent shrinkage. Those who want to grow their brains should engage in a new activity and repeat it until it becomes a new skill. This can take anywhere from 18 days to 254 days. Each new activity that becomes a skill creates brain mass and keeps your mind active and your brain healthy.

Weight Training Three or More Days a Week

Neural stem cells (new brain cells) are born in the hippocampus and either divide into neural cells or glial cells (support cells for neurons). Neural cells are sent from the hippocampus to the dendrite gyrus, which acts like a traffic cop, ordering them to go to specific regions of the brain. Voluntary exercise increases the number of neural stem cells created by the hippocampus. Here's how it works: weight training delivers blood-soaked oxygen to the brain. The more you lift weights, the higher the blood flow. This increased blood flow then feeds the brain with more glucose (brain fuel) and oxygen (which removes free radicals from the brain like a sponge, in effect cleaning the brain). Weight training also increases the production of BDNF (Brain Derived Neurotrophic Factor) inside the hippocampus. BDNF is like miracle grow for the brain, helping it give birth to more brain cells (neurons). BDNF also helps increase the health and size of old neurons. In effect, weight training grows your brain by creating new brain cells and also helps maintain the health of old brain cells. Every brain cell has one axon and multiple dendrites. The axon of each brain cell connects with the dendrites of other brain cells. This is called a synapse. There is a direct correlation between the number of axons and synapses an individual has and his/her intelligence. Lifting weights increases the growth of axons, which helps contribute to increased synaptic activity. Anything that increases the number of axons and synapses, therefore, increases intelligence.

Powerful, Relationship-Building Habits

Self-made millionaires are very particular about who they associate with. Their goal is to develop relationships with other success-minded individuals. In Smart Money Principle #12, I will teach you the difference between Rich Relationships and Toxic Relationships.

Self-made millionaires use four relationship building strategies to grow and strengthen their relationships:

1. Hello Call–The Hello Call is used primarily to gather critical information on each contact, which helps you grow your relationships.
2. Happy Birthday Call–The Happy Birthday Call keeps your relationships on life support. At least once a year you are forced to reach out to your contacts to wish them a happy birthday. About five to ten percent of these contacts will reciprocate and

call you on your birthday, taking your relationship off life support.

3. Life Event Call–The Life Event Call is the most powerful relationship-building strategy. This is a call you make to acknowledge some emotional life event: birth, death, engagement, marriage, health issue, etc. Life event calls grow the roots to the relationship tree deeper and faster than any other relationship-building strategy.

4. Networking/Volunteering–Networking & Volunteering allows you to meet new people and offers the opportunity to showcase your skills in a safe, friendly and stress-free environment. Developing a networking process is critical to success. When you network the right way, you gain customers, clients, strategic business partners, followers, and networking partners and this translates into more money. Self-made millionaires are master networkers. Their networking efforts are intended to grow their association with other successful or success-minded individuals. There are a number of ways these millionaires go about networking. They join networking groups, advisory boards of community businesses, local civic groups and local community-based non-profits. The non-profit groups are particularly useful. They offer an opportunity for you to showcase your skills and knowledge and provide an opportunity to help you build relationships with other successful people, who always seem to populate the boards of non-profits.

Smart Money Principle #2 – Choose Your Spouse Wisely

Tom and Margaret O'Neill had the same values, the same habits, the same dreams and goals in life. They were aligned in their thinking. They were true partners. The Veblins were often on the wrong page with each other. Joan deferred to John on the honeymoon. John deferred to Joan on the private education for their kids. Who you marry can lift you up or drag you down. Despite what you may have read in the romance novels or seen in the movies, you can fall in love with anyone. There is no one person out there for you. Finding a spouse who shares your work ethic, financial goals and life plan is crucial to success. So how do you find the perfect mate? You begin by defining your ideal spouse. Besides looks, define the ideal characteristics you want in a future spouse:

- What's Their Mental Outlook? – Are they positive, optimistic, enthusiastic, etc?
- What's Their Work Ethic? Are they hard working or lazy?
- What's Their Level of Education?
- What's Their Attitude About Lifelong Learning? Are they readers? Do they like to learn new, novel things?
- How Do They Feel About Money?
- Are They Frugal About Spending Money?
- Are They Savers?
- Are They Risk Averse?
- Are They Charitable?
- Are They Supportive?

- Do They Have a Life Plan? What's their life plan look like? Does it match your life plan?
- Do They Like to Travel?
- Do They Love Kids?
- Do They Ever Get Depressed?
- Do They Drink Alcohol? If so, how much?
- Are They Health Conscious? Do they exercise regularly?
- Do They Have Dreams and Goals? What are their dreams and goals in life?
- Who Are their Friends? Who is in their inner circle? How well do you know the people inside their inner circle?

If you don't know the type of person you want to marry, you could end up spending your life with someone who does not share your values, dreams, goals, or life plan. Remember, success is a process. A big part of that process is who you surround yourself with. Make sure you surround yourself with individuals who share your values, habits, thinking, dreams, and goals.

Smart Money Principle #3 – Avoid Want Spending

Tom O'Neill could have bought the expensive engagement ring, but he chose not to. Tom and Margaret could have splurged on an expensive wedding, but they chose not to. Tom and Margaret could have gone on an exotic honeymoon, but they chose not to. The Veblins, on the other hand, gave into want spending.

Want spenders surrender to instant gratification, eschewing saving in order to buy things they want now: exotic vacations, expensive cars, bigger homes, jewelry, boats, etc. Want spenders spend too much money at bars and restaurants. Worse, they incur debt in order to finance their high standard of living. Want spenders create their own poverty. They are undisciplined with their money. When want spenders are no longer able to work due to old age or disability, they live out the remainder of their lives in abject poverty. They become dependent on family, friends, the government or the charity of others. Their poverty is the byproduct of a Poor Habit known as want spending.

Want spending is a Poor Habit fueled by envy. When you are envious, you want what others have, even if you can't afford it. The non-rich want what the rich have. So, they engage in want spending in order to satisfy their envy. This is one of the main reasons credit card debt has exploded among the non-rich.

What shuts off want spending's fuel, is gratitude. Gratitude is the gateway to a positive mental outlook and the salve which cures the Poor Habit of want spending. When you are grateful for what you have, you no longer envy what others have. But gratitude, like envy, is a mental habit that must first be forged before it does its magic. Once you forge that habit, gratitude stops want spending in its tracks.

If you want to save money, you must put an end to want spending. How? Every morning, express gratitude for three things that went right in your life the day before:

1. My car started, and I am grateful.
2. My air conditioner worked, and I am grateful.
3. Someone said something nice to me, and I am grateful.

This morning routine helps reprogram your thinking from negative (envy) to positive (gratitude). Within a few weeks, you will start to see things differently. Positivity will replace negativity. Your glass will begin to be seen as half-filled, not half-empty.

Smart Money Principle #4 – Be Frugal, Not Cheap

The O'Neills were frugal with their money. Tom brought his lunch to work. The O'Neills found an inexpensive apartment in Hoboken. Margaret used coupons to buy groceries and shopped for clothing at Goodwill stores. The Veblins were not frugal. They did not think about how they spent their money.

Being frugal requires three things:
1. Awareness – Being aware of how you spend your money.
2. Quality – Spending your money on quality products and services.
3. Bargain Shopping – Spending the least amount possible by shopping around for the lowest price.

Self –made millionaire Saver-Investors are frugal when it comes to spending their money. They know where their money is going. This gives them control over their money. You'll never get rich if you spend more than you make.

Frugal Smart Money Habits

- Use Coupons – Even the wealthy in my Rich Habits Study engaged in this money savings habit. Thirty percent of the rich in my study used coupons to buy food. Why pay more than you have to on groceries or other expenses?

- Keep Your Home or Apartment Small – For most, a home or apartment is the most expensive part of the spending budget. When you keep the size of your home or apartment small, it will reduce how much you spend in mortgage interest, rent, real estate taxes, repairs, utilities and insurance. Strive to keep your housing costs below twenty-five percent of your monthly net pay.

- Bargain Shop – Far too many make spontaneous purchases, paying much more than they otherwise would. That's a Poor Habit. Shopping for bargains and taking advantage of sales events are smart money habits.
- Stick to BYOBs – There are many restaurants that do not sell alcohol, beer or wine and allow you to bring your own spirit of choice into their restaurant. Restaurants markup liquor sales by as much as one hundred percent, so BYOBs save you money.
- Keep Vacation Costs Low – Spend less than five percent of your net income on vacations. Self-made millionaires do not go on exotic vacations. They take modest, inexpensive vacations. They find bargain vacation deals for their family.
- Food Budget – Spend less than fifteen percent of your net income on food.
- Entertainment Budget – Spend less than ten percent of your net income on entertainment/gifts. This category includes bars, restaurants, movies, music, books, gifts, etc. Eating out and any prepared food you purchase is part of your entertainment budget.
- Cars – Spend less than five percent of your net income on car expenses. Car expenses include monthly car payment, car insurance, gas, tolls, registration fees, repairs and maintenance.
- Never Gamble – Gambling is high-risk speculation. It is a tax on the poor.

- Clothing – Spend less than five percent of your net income on clothing. Many Goodwill stores carry high quality clothing. You may have to spend a few extra bucks on tailoring, but it is well worth the additional cost.

Maintain a spending budget for all of the above spending categories and get into the habit of writing down everything you spend for thirty days. This will open your eyes to how much you actually spend. Real spending is always a very different dollar amount than imagined spending. You will be shocked to find out how much you spend on certain budget categories. And that's a good thing. Getting control of your spending is not an easy task. Once it becomes a daily habit, however, it gets much easier. You will fall into a pattern and a routine that will keep you out of the poor house, enable you to save and puts you on the path to financial independence.

One other important point I want to make about being frugal. People often confuse being frugal with being cheap. There's a huge difference between being frugal and being cheap.

Cornelius Vanderbilt, the richest man in the world in the late 1800's, controlled much of America's transportation in two sectors – the steamships and the railroads. He was revered for his ability to minimize costs. His attention to financial details was unsurpassed during his reign. For example, when he took over the New York Central Railroad, one of the first things he did was remove all of the brass from all of the trains. This cost him a lot of money in removing all of the brass from his rail cars. People thought he was crazy.

Why did he do it?

Brass needed to be polished every day. No brass meant no more need to pay people to polish it every day. Eliminating the expense of polishing the brass far and away exceeded the cost of its removal, saving his railroad companies an enormous amount of money in the long run.

Frugal and cheap have nothing in common. Frugal spending means buying the highest quality product or service, at the lowest price. Cheap spending means buying the cheapest product or service, with little to no regard for quality. Cheap spending is a Poor Habit because you ignore quality and, instead, wind up purchasing cheap, poor quality products or services.

Cheap products break down after just a few years, forcing you to replace those products over and over again.

Cheap services are typically provided by those who are either inexperienced in their field, or who are not very good at what they do. This lack of experience or lack of competence can result in mistakes that cost you money down the road.

The costs of cheap spending are one of those taxes the non-rich pay that the rich don't pay.

On its own, being frugal will not make you rich. It is just one piece to the Rich Habits puzzle, and there are many pieces. Frugal Spending will enable you to increase the amount of money you can save. The more you are able to save, the more you'll have to invest. Having money set aside in savings allows you to take advantage of investment opportunities. Without savings, those opportunities pass you by.

Smart Money Principle #5 – Avoid Spontaneous Spending

The O'Neills did not spend money recklessly. They were very disciplined about their spending. The Veblins, on the other hand, were reckless with their spending. They lacked discipline. They had the spontaneous spending Poor Habit.

Spontaneous spending is driven by four factors:
1. Emotions – When you feel very optimistic about the future, you could find yourself engaging in spontaneous spending. You assume the future will be brighter and that your income will increase every year. When you allow emotional highs to influence your thinking, you can fall into the trap of spontaneously spending your income, eschewing it for savings. When you feel sad or depressed, spontaneous purchases can act like a temporary salve, lifting you from momentary sadness. The remedy is to be constantly vigilant regarding your emotions. Be like Spock – control your emotions. This keeps your prefrontal cortex in control of your brain and prevents the emotional part of your brain from making spending decisions.
2. Decision Fatigue – Everyone has about three hours of willpower energy. Willpower energy is most abundant after a good night's sleep. When willpower is high, your prefrontal cortex is in complete control of your brain. When willpower is low, your prefrontal cortex weakens and this reduces your control over your spending. This is why supermarkets place

products at the checkout lines. They know that you have depleted your willpower reserves and that you are suffering from decision fatigue. Their hope is, in your weakened state, you'll make a spontaneous purchase. The remedy is to shop immediately upon waking up from a night's sleep, after taking a nap, or after a light meal. These three things restore your willpower reserves.

3. Inner Circle – If those inside your inner circle suffer from poor spending habits, they will infect you with their habits. You will find yourself emulating their habits and, thus, their behaviors, thoughts and emotions. The remedy is to change who is in your inner circle, from spenders to savers.

4. Impairment – Drugs and alcohol impair your thinking and lead to spending mistakes. Never spend money when you are impaired. The remedy is to wait until the effects of the drugs or alcohol fade, before making any spending decisions, or, to avoid impairment altogether.

Smart Money Principle #6 – Be The Architect of Your Life–Have a Blueprint or Plan

The O'Neills had a plan. Their plan was to save and invest their way to wealth. The Veblins did not have any plan.

You need to create a blueprint for your ideal, future life. This is called Dream-Setting. Dream-Setting is the act of defining the life of your dreams, in the form of a script or narrative.

It involves a four-step process:

1. Future Letter – Go into the future five, ten or even twenty years. Then write down every detail about your ideal future life. Be very specific: the significant income you earn each year, the fulfilling work you do to earn that income, the amazing house you live in, the dream car you drive, the influential people you associate with, the significant wealth you've accumulated, exotic places you've traveled to, etc. Also, explain what you did during the years in order to get where you are in your future life. Share all of the goals you achieved and the dreams you realized. List all of your accomplishments.

2. List Every Dream – Using the future letter, make a bullet point list of each one of the details that represent your ideal life. These would be the income you earn, the house you live in, etc. These details represent your dreams, which will become the blueprint of your ideal, future life.

3. Build Goals Around Each Dream – In order to realize a given dream, it may require that you accomplish

numerous goals. Once you accomplish those goals, your dream will be realized.

4. Create Goal Habits – The final step requires that you forge daily habits (goal habits) that, when accomplished each day, brings you closer to achieving each individual goal. Once you complete all of the goals around one dream, you realize that dream and then move on to the next dream.

Each dream realized is like climbing a rung on your ladder to your future life. When you realize all of your dreams, when you get to the top of that ladder, you have arrived – you are living the life of your dreams.

Thanks to their blueprint, the O'Neills arrived at the top of their ladder in their early fifties.

Smart Money Principle #7 – Consistently Invest Your Savings

The O'Neills put their savings to work. They prudently invested their savings. Saving is important, because without saving, you cannot invest those savings and grow your wealth.

Most people have one stream of income – their jobs. And most people are either poor or stuck in the middle-class. If you want to break out of poverty or the middle-class, you need to save in order to help you create multiple streams of income. Every single self-made millionaire in my Rich Habits Study started with one stream of income. Then they added a second, then a third and so on.

Why is this so important? When one stream is negatively affected by economic downturns or some unexpected life event, such as a disability, the other streams can come to the rescue and help you survive the downturn or life event without dramatically affecting your lifestyle.

How do you create multiple streams of income? It's a two-step process:

1. Live Below Your Means So You Can Save – Save twenty percent or more of your net income every year and learn to live off the remaining amount. Saving first forces you to reduce your standard of living in order to live off what remains.
2. Prudently Invest Your Savings – Invest your savings into productive assets that generate additional income streams. Examples include:
    - Residential or Commercial Rental Properties– Rental Income Stream.

- Seasonal Rental Properties such as Beach Rentals, Ski Resort Rentals, Lake Front Rentals–Seasonal Rental Income Stream.
- Stocks–Dividends and Capital Gains Streams.
- Bonds–Interest Income Stream.
- Mutual Funds–Dividends, Interest and Capital Gains Streams.
- Annuities–Future Retirement Income Stream.
- Permanent Life Insurance–Cash Surrender Value or Accelerated Death Benefits Streams.
- Timber, Oil and Gas–Royalty Income Stream.

Smart Money Principle #8 – Invest Prudently

Tom and Margaret O'Neill invested their savings in stocks that they studied for many months before investing. If you recall, Margaret and Tom would reach out to their Financial Advisor for stock recommendations. They would then ask their advisor to send them detailed financials on a particular company or about a particular mutual fund. Only after they were done studying a company or mutual fund, would they reach out to their financial advisor to make the purchase. They also invested their savings in real estate in the town in which they lived. They invested only in things they knew a lot about. They did their homework before making any investment.

This is known as Educated Risk. The rich significantly reduce the risks associated with investing by doing their homework. They study investments for many months before deciding to invest any of their money. They eschew get rich quick schemes or fad investing.

The non-rich don't do their homework. They don't study investments. They take uneducated risk. The non-rich have a get-rich-quick mindset. They look for ways to accumulate wealth very quickly, without the work. The get-rich-quick mindset brainwashes the non-rich into believing that there is an easier path towards accumulating wealth, one in which you are not required to do the requisite heavy lifting, that financial success always requires.

Those with a get-rich-quick mindset do not pursue their dreams. They do not set goals. They do not step outside their comfort zone, experimenting and learning new things.

They do not engage in daily self-improvement as a whetstone in developing expert knowledge or skills.

Smart Money Principle #9 – Make Your Money Invisible

Margaret and Tom had a system, or process that enabled them to save money every time Tom received a paycheck. Margaret would immediately deposit some of their income into a savings account and she did this with every paycheck. She automated their savings, which forced them to live off of the remaining money in their checking account. They then put their savings to work by investing it, initially in stocks, and later on in rental properties in Manasquan.

The O'Neills made their money invisible by immediately and consistently putting a certain amount of Tom's income into a savings account and then investing that money, as soon as they could.

Today, it's much easier to automate the savings and investment process. You can have part of every paycheck sent to your savings account electronically.

Smart Money Principle #10 – Avoid Lifestyle Creep and Don't Supersize Your Life

The O'Neills lived in an inexpensive apartment in Hoboken. They ate at inexpensive restaurants. They went on inexpensive vacations. They purchased their cars and kept them for many years. They sent their kids to public school. They surrounded themselves with other frugal-minded individuals to help keep them on track.

Conversely, the Veblins lived in an expensive apartment in New York City. They bought new cars every three years. They bought boats. They went on expensive vacations. They sent their kids to expensive private schools. They ate out several times a week at expensive restaurants. They surrounded themselves with other non-frugal individuals.

The definition of Lifestyle Creep is: ***To increase your standard of living in order to match your increased income.***

It's a common Poor Habit among many who suddenly find themselves making more money. In the early days of human existence, it was feast or famine. During very rare periods of food abundance, ancient humans would take immediate advantage of this abundance and gorge themselves. Doing so enabled early humans to build up significant stores of fat. When food scarcity returned, early humans were then able to survive by living off those stores of fat accumulated during the periods of food abundance.

This instant gratification trait is still with us today. During periods of financial abundance, humans are evolutionarily hardwired to gorge themselves, or spend money, when money is available on things like bigger homes, luxury cars, jewelry, swimming pools, expensive vacations, etc.

The Rich Habit is to delay gratification by choosing to forgo this innate spending impulse so you can put that money into your savings and investments to fund your future standard of living.

Therefore, when you receive a raise, bonus, promotion or higher-paying job, don't supersize your life by purchasing a bigger home, expensive cars, jewelry or any other stuff. Save that increase in income for your future self. One way to do this is to commit to saving a percentage of your income, including raises and bonuses. This way you stick to a consistent savings plan that will benefit the future you.

Once you spend your money, it's gone. When you hit a bump in the road, such as a job loss or disability, you are then forced to sell your stuff. If the stuff you purchased depreciated in value, you get pennies on the dollar.

If you want to **guarantee** that you will one day become financially independent, you must develop the habit of keeping your standard of living modest. You force yourself to do this by automatically saving twenty percent or more of your income and prudently investing your savings. When you save twenty percent or more of your income, this forces you to reduce your standard of living, in order to be able to live off the remaining income. Given enough time, your investments will make you financially independent or, perhaps, even wealthy.

One of the self-made millionaires in my study who followed this Saver-Investor path explained to me his simple rule for financial success: ***Same house, same spouse, same car.***

There's a lot of wisdom in these words. What they really mean is that no matter what good fortune visits you in life, do not change your standard of living. Don't supersize your life by buying things you really do not need. Live a modest life and save and invest for your future self.

Smart Money Principle #11 – Be Open Minded and Don't Let Limiting Beliefs Dictate Your Financial Decisions

Joan Veblin had a bias against public schools, which manifested itself in their decision to send their kids to private school. She was not open-minded about the Manasquan public school system.

What causes a closed mind?

- Ideology – Unwavering beliefs that have locked in your thinking. Most of these beliefs are inherited from your upbringing. Sometimes, they are adopted from the thinking of influencers or significant others. Ideology, when it goes unchallenged, acts like a wall, blocking out any challenges to your thinking.
- Ignorance – When you lack knowledge, you are unable to see opportunities when they present themselves.
- Overactive Ego – Having an overactive ego means you think you are always right. This closes your mind to new information, ideas and facts that could be critical to your success.
- Low Self-Esteem – When you have low self-esteem, you undervalue your own thoughts, ideas and personal power. Low self-esteem is like a self-manufactured braking system that stops you in your tracks, preventing you from moving forward.
- Anger/Hatred – Anger and hatred are two very costly negative emotions that consumes your thinking and your actions. When you are angry with someone or

hate someone, you ignore what he/she has to say. Anger and hatred closes your mind.

It's no coincidence that self-made millionaires have made it a habit to be open-minded. Being open-minded is a prerequisite for success. The embrace of new ideas, information and knowledge requires an open mind. You simply cannot learn and grow as an individual if your mind is closed to the ideas of others. Yet most people are closed-minded, embracing certain ideologies and limiting beliefs that make it virtually impossible for them to grow and prosper. Being closed-minded limits your opportunities in life and stunts your growth, consigning you to a fate of mediocrity, poverty, or failure. Being open-minded clears the path for unlimited opportunity and growth.

Embrace new ideas, even if they initially challenge your sensibilities. Don't ever close your mind to the ideas of others, no matter how outside your comfort zone those ideas may make you feel. Open-mindedness is not innate or an inborn human trait. It has to be forged, like a habit. That is why it is one of my many Rich Habits. Those who are open-minded grow. Those who are closed-minded do not grow and become stuck in life.

Money Smart Principle #12 – Surround Yourself With Other Savers

Tom and Margaret associated with friends who shared their habit of living a frugal lifestyle. They went out to restaurants with these friends. The Veblins associated with individuals who, like them, enjoyed dining at expensive restaurants.

Like attracts Like. Unconsciously, we seek to associate with others who are like us.

According to Nicolas Christakas, a former Yale University researcher, habits spread like a virus throughout your social networks.

This could be a good thing, if the things you have in common are constructive and improve your life. For example, if your inner circle includes people who are thrifty and focused on saving money, it's highly likely you'll be infected by their smart money habits.

It could also be a bad thing, however, if the habits of your inner circle are destructive or toxic. According to my Rich Habits Study, those struggling financially in life unintentionally surrounded themselves with toxic relationships – negative individuals with bad money habits, bad health habits, emotional instability, addictions, poor work ethic, and many other things detrimental to living happy, successful lives.

Conversely, the self-made millionaires in my Rich Habits Study intentionally surrounded themselves with Rich Relationships – upbeat individuals with smart money habits, good health habits, emotional stability, and strong, long-term relationships with similar or like-minded people.

For those who want to improve the quality of their lives, it is very important to pursue rich relationships as members of your inner circle, or insider's club, and minimize your exposure to toxic relationships. Forging rich relationships and avoiding toxic relationships is a science or process. At the heart of that process is understanding the difference between rich relationships and toxic relationships.

Rich Relationship Traits

The hallmark of these individuals is an upbeat, optimistic, positive mental outlook. Rich relationship types have a can-do attitude. They believe individuals can accomplish anything they put their mind to.

Rich relationships lift you up. They open doors that are otherwise closed. They help you solve your problems, achieve your goals and realize your dreams. When they are part of your inner circle, they improve your life. They drip words of happiness, love, and encouragement on you, which helps keep you moving forward in the pursuit of your goals and dreams.

Here are some of the traits of rich relationships:

- Abundance Mindset – They don't see success as a zero sum game, meaning for every winner there must be a loser. They believe everyone can win.
- Solutions-Focused – They are focused on finding solutions to problems.
- Provide Constructive Criticism – They offer criticism that is intended to help others, not demean or discourage them.

142

- Optimistic – They believe they can change the circumstances of their lives.
- Confident – They take action on their goals and dreams, which boosts their confidence.
- Humble – They see egotism as a deficiency.
- Emotionally Stable – They intentionally control their emotions, especially when things go wrong in life. This gives others confidence in doing business with them.
- Can-Do Attitude – They believe they are the architects of their lives.
- Happy – They look for the good in life, not the bad.
- Grateful – They focus on what they have, not on what others have.
- You First-Me Later – They focus on adding value to the lives of others and putting the needs of others ahead of their own.
- Patient – They understand success and wealth takes a long time.
- Relentlessly Persistent – They never quit on their goals and dreams.
- Focused on the Future – They are consistently pursuing goals and dreams.
- Seek Feedback From Others – They seek feedback as a means to help them pivot and improve upon what they are doing.
- Authentic – They do not pretend to be someone they are not. This is because they like who they are.
- Long-Term Focused – They invest in themselves, sacrificing today for a brighter future.

Toxic Relationship Traits

The hallmark of members of this group is pessimism and a negative mental outlook. Toxic relationship-types see themselves as victims of their circumstances. This negative, victim outlook fosters a sense of entitlement – they believe they were wronged and someone should right that wrong. Typically, that someone is government. They see various elements of society as holding them back, making it impossible for them to lift themselves out of their poverty or financial struggles. They blame their parents, Wall Street, the rich, banks, government policies or society in general for their financial woes. They rarely blame themselves.

Toxic relationships will drag you down. Their lives are filled with drama, conflict, put out the fire-type emergencies and financial struggle. When they are in your orbit, their problems eventually become your problems.

Here are some of the traits of Toxic Relationships:

- Financial Problems – Toxic people have money problems. They have significant debt, typically credit card debt. They borrow money from individuals they know in order to put out fires. If they are part of your inner circle, eventually they will call upon you to lend them money.
- Scarcity Mindset – They believe wealth is scarce and difficult, if not impossible, to acquire.
- Problems-Focused – They are focused on finding problems rather than solutions to their problems. They see problems everywhere.

- Destructive Criticism – Because they have low self-esteem, they seek to drag others down along with them by using pejorative and critical language.
- Pessimistic – They see no future or a very limited future. As a result, they are reluctant to pursue their goals and dreams.
- Exaggerated Ego – They have a bad habit of inflating themselves in the presence of others in order to impress people.
- Uncontrolled Emotions – They allow their emotions to run wild. They are quick to anger.
- Helpless/Hopeless – They have lost hope in their ability to lift themselves up and improve their lives.
- Sad/Depressed – They have a morbid outlook on life, and this makes them feel sad and even depressed.
- Wanting – They only see what they lack. They are not grateful for what they have. They are always looking at what other people have and making comparisons.
- Me First-You Last – Their entitlement mindset puts their needs and wants ahead of others.
- Impatient – Their lack of a long-term focus on building wealth, coupled with a sense of helplessness regarding their lives, makes them impatient for change.
- Fear of Feedback – Because they are insecure or struggle with an exaggerated ego, they avoid seeking feedback from others. In fact, they fear and avoid feedback.

- Fake – They are unhappy about the circumstances of their lives and their ego drives them to pretend to be someone they are not.
- Short-Term Focused – They seek immediate gratification and are unwilling to invest in themselves for the long-term. They want what they want and they want it now.

Your goal should be to create your own unique insider's club comprised of individuals who possess smart money habits and other rich relationship traits. When you know what traits to be on the lookout for, it's easy to separate rich relationship types from toxic types.

Rich relationships will help you pull your cart. They will become active participants in your journey towards building wealth. They will be your greatest assets.

Smart Money Principle #13 – Save For What Matters Most To You

Tom and Margaret had certain values that helped them create smart money habits. They saved money so they could put more money down on their homes. They saved money so they could invest their savings in order to create multiple streams of income. They saved money for their kids' college so they could fund their college education. Saving money for their homes, saving money so they could build multiple streams of income, and saving money for college were what the O'Neills valued most. They did not place any value on acquiring possessions in order to impress others.

The Veblins, on the other hand, had very different values. They placed a high value on living large and impressing people with their home, their vacations, their jewelry, their boats, and many other meaningless possessions. They preferred to live for today. Instant gratification drove almost every financial decision they made. Their values did not allow them to save for their kids' college education, their retirement, or for unexpected consequences.

What are values? Values are things in life that are most important to you. What is most important to you becomes a priority in your life and you will devote significant time and money to those priorities. For me, being a caring, loving and mentoring dad and grandad was my number one priority. Even though my kids are adults now, I still carve time out of my very busy schedule to spend time with them. I do this because my family is my priority.

What do you value? What's important to you? Knowledge, compassion, family, financial security, friendship, honesty, generosity, mentoring, self-improvement, spirituality, wealth, happiness, power, philanthropy, respect, leadership, love, living a simple life, good habits?

Values, like habits, spread like a virus to your inner circle. When those values are good values, they benefit those inside your inner circle also. Values help shape your life and the lives of those around you, good or bad.

Values are major pillars that act like a foundation for the life you live. They are the things that are most important to you. As an example, my values, in their order of importance, would be:

- Immediate Family
- Good Health
- Friendships
- Rich Relationships
- Learning
- Financial Security
- Mentoring Others
- Extended Family

Your values are important because your values are drivers – they set in motion other things like your dreams, the vision of your ideal life, passions and habits.

I've come to realize, thanks to my research, that values give birth to the habits we adopt in life. As an example, because of my values, I've adopted the following habits:

- Frequent Hello Calls to my kids (Immediate Family), my friends (Friendship), my brothers, sisters and in-laws (Extended Family) and other specific

relationships I would like to grow or maintain (Rich Relationships).
- Exercise every day and eat a lot of vegetables in order to maintain healthy microbiota (Good Health).
- Daily reading (Learning).
- Writing books about my Rich Habits (Mentoring Others).

Therefore, if you have good values, you'll forge Rich Habits and those Rich Habits will create a good life. Conversely, if you have bad values, you'll forge Poor Habits and your life will be miserable.

When your values are off, your habits will be off and your life will be off.

Your habits are really nothing more than daily repetitive activities built around your values. Your habits are your values in motion. Define what is truly most important to you. Don't put any value on possessions. Possessions will not make you happy. Financial freedom will make you happy.

Smart Money Principle #14 – Money Equals Freedom

Because the O'Neills saved and invested their savings wisely, Tom was able to leave his law firm and spend more time with his family. Their savings habit also enabled Tom to retire in his early fifties.

When John became disabled, the Veblins were forced to move out of the home they loved. They were dependent on the generosity of others to survive. Because of their poor money habits, they lost the ability to choose what they did with their lives. Their poor money habits, in effect, cost them their freedom.

Smart Money Principle #15 – Good Health is Critical to Financial Success

Tom O'Neill exercised every day in order to improve his health. John Veblin did not exercise at all and became overweight. This eventually destroyed his health.

You can't make money from a hospital bed. Being healthy is a prerequisite for building wealth. And daily exercise, especially aerobic exercise, keeps you healthy in a number of ways:

- Aerobic exercise increases blood flow to the brain, feeding the body with oxygen-rich blood.
- Aerobic exercise strengthens your heart.
- Aerobic exercise helps to widen your small blood vessels (capillaries) in order to help absorb the increased oxygen. This oxygen is then carried to your muscles and every cell in your body. The oxygen also carries away waste products, such as free radicals and lactic acid.
- When you exercise aerobically, your body releases endorphins, which are natural painkillers that pro-mote an increased sense of well-being.
- Aerobic exercise reduces the risk of obesity, heart disease, high blood pressure, type 2 diabetes, stroke and certain types of cancer.
- Weight-bearing aerobic exercises, such as walking or jogging, reduce the risk of osteoporosis.
- Aerobic exercise helps lower blood sugar.
- Aerobic exercise boosts your high-density lipopro-tein (HDL or "good cholesterol") and lowers your low-density lipoprotein (LDL or "bad cholesterol").

The potential result? Less buildup of plaques in your arteries.

- People who engage in regular aerobic exercise, live longer and are therefore more productive than those who don't exercise regularly. This increased productivity magnifies the amount of income you can create during your lifetime.

Smart Money Principle #16 – Create Multiple Streams of Income

The O'Neills used their savings from Tom's salary to create multiple streams of income. Their stock investments created dividend and capital gains income. Their numerous real estate investments created several streams of rental income. They saved part of their income in order to create future retirement income.

The Veblins relied on only one source of income – John's salary. When John became disabled, they had no other revenue streams to come to the rescue.

Expanding and diversifying your sources of income enables you to weather the economic downturns that always occur. These downturns are not as severe to the wealthy as they are to those with one stream of income, typically their jobs.

The non-rich have "one pole in one pond" and when that single income stream is impacted by an economic downturn or something unexpected, like becoming disabled, the non-rich suffer financially.

When you have one revenue stream, you are not in control of your life. Outside forces, like a recession or disability can pull the rug out from underneath your feet very quickly.

The rich have "several poles in many ponds" and they are able to draw income from other sources when one source is temporarily impaired.

Some of the additional streams the rich in my study invested in included:
- Real estate rentals.

- REITs.
- Tenants-in-common real estate investments.
- Triple net leases.
- Stock market investments and mutual funds.
- Annuities.
- Seasonal real estate rentals (beach rentals, ski rentals, lakefront rentals).
- Private equity investments.
- Part ownership in side businesses.
- Royalties (patents, books, oil, timber, etc.).

Smart Money Principle #17 – Wealth Isn't Just About Money – 7 Types of Wealth

The O'Neills had multiple types of wealth. They had financial wealth, health wealth, relationship wealth, time wealth, and peace of mind wealth. They created each type of wealth themselves. Remember that Tom even changed jobs in order to be able to spend more time with his family.

The Veblins did not create multiple types of wealth. They struggled financially, John lost his health, and until the day they passed away, they worried about money.

When you think about the word "wealth" what immediately comes to mind? Money or investments probably.

When I finished my Rich Habits Study, it occurred to me that there were many habits of the rich that seemed completely unrelated to the accumulation of money. Thanks to my study, I discovered the seven types of wealth:

1. Financial Wealth – Having more money than you need to live the life you want to live.
2. Health Wealth – Lean, healthy, and physically fit, with the absence of any chronic diseases.
3. Relationship Wealth – Surrounded by an abundance of upbeat, optimistic, happy people who love you, care about you and who encourage and support everything you do.
4. Time Wealth – Having enough free, non-work time to spend with family and friends and to do the things you like to do.
5. Intellectual Wealth – Possessing expert knowledge that you put to use in providing an income for you and your family or to benefit others.

6. Talent Wealth – Possessing unique talents that you put to use in providing an income for you and your family or to benefit others.
7. Peace of Mind Wealth – Little to no stress. Feeling calm and relaxed.

Wealth isn't always about money. There are many ways you can be rich.

Smart Money Principle #18 – Becoming Rich Isn't an Event

Becoming rich isn't an event, it's a process. And, for the Saver-Investors in my Rich Habits Study, that process takes time.

The O'Neills had a process that enabled them to build their wealth. They consistently saved part of Tom's paycheck and then prudently invested their savings over many, many years. In order to save, they were forced to make certain sacrifices that helped them reduce their cost of living. Eventually, their consistent smart money habits produced an enormous amount of wealth.

The Veblins had no process other than John working until he reached full retirement age so that he could then become the beneficiary of his company's generous pension plan. Essentially, John put all of his eggs in one basket – the pension plan.

The O'Neills, over many years, diversified their wealth. They invested in stocks and mutual funds. They created equity in their homes and rental properties. They invested in real estate in Manasquan. This took time, but by diversifying their wealth, the O'Neills created multiple streams of income that eventually made them very wealthy.

Smart Money Principle #19 – Good Goals Verses Bad Goals

The O'Neills set good goals. They consistently saved a portion of Tom's income and then prudently invested those savings. They saved for their kids' college education. They built up enormous equity in all of the homes they owned, which lowered how much they had to pay to the bank every month for their mortgage. The reduced mortgage helped to lower their monthly cost of living and Tom was then free to leave his law firm for a lower-paying, less-demanding job.

The Veblins set bad goals: a big engagement ring, expensive wedding, an exotic honeymoon, opulent Manasquan home, lavish vacations and John's boating obsession. They spent their money in order to fund bad goals.

Not all goals are good goals. You need to understand the difference between good goals and bad goals.

Good Goals

Good goals are long-term focused. They forgo instant gratification or immediate rewards in order to generate benefits down the road. These benefits should include financial independence, good health, long-term, valuable relationships and happiness. Good goals benefit the future you. They push you to grow and improve, so that you become the individual you desire to be in the future.

An example of a good goal would be to lose twenty pounds. Setting a weight-loss goal often involves a daily regimen of exercise, healthy eating and embracing a healthy lifestyle. Good health results from exercising and eating right. It may also motivate you to moderate your consumption of alcohol or to quit smoking. When the weight eventually comes off, you enjoy the compliments and feel healthier, which creates long-term happiness.

Bad Goals

Bad goals are short-term focused. They forgo delayed gratification in order to create immediate benefits, ignoring the impact on your future self. Bad goals ignore the future. They do not help you grow or improve as an individual.

An example of a bad goal would be to own a Ferrari. In order to own a Ferrari, you decide you need to make more money. Making more money will likely involve either more work or taking excessive financial risk (i.e. gambling). There's a cost-benefit to working more – you see less of your family. Don't misunderstand me here. Working more to make more money can be a good thing. But where the goal goes south is when you then invest that extra money in possessions, like a Ferrari.

The happiness you derive from owning more or better things will fade over time, since happiness derived from buying anything is always short term. You will eventually revert back to your genetic happiness baseline and, after a few weeks, the Ferrari will no longer create lasting happiness. The lost time with the family, however, can never be recouped.

If the goal, instead, was to judiciously invest that extra money you earned into a calculated risk, such as a side business, stock investments or a real estate rental investment, then it transforms the "make more money" goal into a good goal.

The benefits of achieving a goal should create some long-term benefit or result in long-term happiness: more time with the family, more personal growth, financial independence, improved health, etc. When the achievement of a goal is predicated on owning more possessions or instant gratification, it's almost always a bad goal – a wasted investment.

Be careful of the goals you pursue. Not all goals are created equal.

Smart Money Principle #20 – Good Habits Good Luck – Bad Habits Bad Luck

The O'Neills had good, solid values. They forged habits around those values; habits that helped them realize the goals and dreams that were aligned with their values. Their good habit of saving money in order to achieve financial independence gave Tom the freedom to leave his demanding law firm position for a less-demanding one at a big pharmaceutical company. That company would eventually be bought out and Tom received a lucrative retirement package and a financial windfall in the form of unrestricted stock worth $1 million.

The Veblins had bad values. Like the O'Neills, they too forged habits around their values. The spent every dollar John earned and had nothing in savings. John had no choice but to continue working grueling hours at his law firm. When John had his stroke, they had no savings to rescue them. They were forced to pull their son out of Notre Dame University and eventually had to sell their Manasquan home.

Good habits create a unique type of good luck called Opportunity Luck. The opportunity luck for the O'Neills was the unanticipated buyout of Tom's company. Because of their good savings and investment habits, Tom had the freedom to leave his law firm and find a job working for a publicly held company. Although he would earn less at his new job, it did come with a package which included the opportunity for stock compensation. Tom did receive stock compensation in the form of restricted stock. When his company was acquired, Tom was able to exercise all of his restricted stock as part of the retirement package they offered him. The O'Neills, because of their good habits, were able to make choices that put themselves in a position to become the recipients of good luck.

Bad habits create a unique type of bad luck called Detrimental Luck. The detrimental luck event for the Veblins was John's stroke. Because they had bad money habits, they had no savings and, thus, John had no choice but to continue working long, grueling hours at his law firm. Because John never forged good health habits, those long hours and the stress associated with his work, eventually damaged his health. The Veblins, because of their bad habits, put themselves in a position to become recipients of bad luck.

Smart Money Principle #21 – Wealth Eliminates 58% of Life's Problems (and Stress)

The O'Neills kept their standard of living very low. Instead of spending their money on stuff, they saved and invested their money. As a result, they were able to cover their monthly expenses and had plenty of money set aside in their investments in the event something unexpected occurred. In short, they had few financial worries.

The Veblins had a very high standard of living. Their Manasquan home was one of the largest in the neighborhood. Their big home required higher repairs and maintenance costs, higher utility costs and higher real estate costs. They also had many other expenses: a pool to maintain, John's Golf Club, John's boating obsession, jewelry costs, expensive vacations and many other things. Because their standard of living costs were so high, John and Joan were living paycheck to paycheck. When something unexpected did occur, such as John's stroke, they found themselves in a world of worry, problems and stress. They had medical expense problems, college funding problems, and housing affordability problems.

Rich or poor, everyone faces common problems. I spent many years studying the rich and the poor in my Rich Habits Study and I found that there were twelve frequent big problems almost everyone has to contend with:

1. Health Problems
2. Financial Problems
3. Family Problems
4. Neighbor Problems
5. Home Repair Problems

6. Car Problems
7. Addiction Problems
8. Job Problems
9. Relationship Problems
10. Death or Disability Problems
11. Time Management Problems
12. Weather Problems

These are all common problems. And these problems create unhappiness for anyone affected by them. The big difference between the rich and the poor, is that the rich are able to easily overcome and eliminate most of these problems and thus, eliminate the unhappiness those problems create.

When I analyzed my study data, I discovered that, out of all of these modern day problems, the rich really only struggle with five:

1. Family Problems
2. Health Problems
3. Time Management Problems
4. Death or Disability Problems and
5. Weather Problems.

If you do the math, that's only forty-two percent of life's problems that the wealthy have to contend with. Or, looking at it another way – being rich eliminates fifty-eight percent of life's major problems. Let's delve into this in a little more detail.

#1 Health Problems

According to my Rich Habits Study data, seventy-six percent of the rich do some form of cardio exercise every day for about thirty minutes. The science on the health benefits of cardio exercise is clear – cardio exercise improves your health and extends your life. But what about cancer? Cancer is fairly democratic in that it plagues the rich and the poor alike. However, studies indicate that a poor diet increases the risk factors associated with cancer. According to my Study, the rich and the poor had very different diets. The rich ate significantly less junk food, consumed significantly less alcohol, avoided fast-food restaurants, and consumed far less sugar than the poor did. On top of all this, the rich have the financial means to secure the best medical care, in the event something does go wrong. Nonetheless, although the rich can afford to find the best medical care available, their money cannot eliminate health problems from occurring.

#2 Financial Problems
The only financial problems the rich have, involves managing their money and investments. One hundred percent of the rich in my study owned their own home and eight-four percent had no mortgage.

#3 Family Problems
Rich or poor, we cannot control family problems. Having a family means you will deal with a whole host of family issues.

#4 Neighbor Problems
The rich have the luxury to pick their neighbors. They can afford to find the best places to live. And if they decide they can't tolerate their neighbors, they have the financial ability to move to a better neighborhood.

#5 Home Repair Problems

If the central air conditioning system breaks, the rich have the money to fix it immediately. When it comes to major repairs, the only issue for the rich is how fast the electrician, plumber, or carpenter can get the job done. There are no financial concerns for the rich when something goes wrong with their home.

#6 Car Problems

If something goes wrong with their car, the rich can afford to get it towed to a repair shop or simply buy a new car.

#7 Addiction Problems

Drugs are a blight on society. No one, not even the rich, can escape this blight. The big difference is that the rich can afford to send themselves, their spouse or their children to the best and most effective rehabilitation centers. The rich have the financial resources to secure the best care in dealing with addiction problems and, therefore, a better chance of eliminating it.

#8 Job Problems

According to my Rich Habits Study data, eighty-six percent of the rich like or love what they do for a living. Because they like or love what they do for a living, they do a better job. They have no fear of being fired because they either own their own business (fifty-one percent of the rich in my study owned their own business) or they are a decision-maker where they work (ninety-one percent in my study were decision-makers), meaning they do the hiring and firing.

#9 Relationship Problems

According to my data, relationships are the currency of the wealthy. The rich surround themselves with other like-minded people who share their goals, dreams, values, thoughts, morality and virtues. They devote an enormous amount of time to managing their relationships and they make a habit of avoiding toxic relationships. Plus, because they are rich, they are treated differently by others. The non-rich, banks, non-profits and many individuals and organizations know that the rich can help them both financially and through their powerful relationships. As a result, the rich are often treated with kid gloves, in the hope that the rich may help them in some way.

#10 Death/Disability Problems

Death or disability can happen to anyone at any time, rich or poor.

#11 Time Management Problems

Sixty-five percent of the rich in my Rich Habits Study had at least three sources of income to manage. As a result, the rich are constantly pressed for time in managing their revenue streams. Plus, according to my Study, ninety-one percent of the rich were decision-makers where they worked. Responsibility follows decision-makers wherever they go, even on vacations. Time management is, therefore, a constant problem for the rich.

#12 Weather Problems

Do I need to even address this? Weather affects everyone, rich or poor.

When you are rich, you can eliminate common, everyday problems and thus, eliminate the unhappiness associated with those problems. When you are poor, these problems linger and often create long-term unhappiness. So, the next time someone tells you money can't buy happiness, don't buy what they're selling.

Far too many have been indoctrinated into the belief that the pursuit of wealth is evil or bad. This belief is a negative or limiting belief and it will hold you back from pursuing wealth. Wealth is good because wealth reduces life's everyday problems.

Smart Money Principle #22 – The Wealth Game Plan

The O'Neills created a blueprint for their lives. They had a wealth game plan. The Veblins did not have a wealth game plan. Instead, without knowing it, they had a poverty game plan. I tried time and time again to help John and Joan change their game plan but they would not listen or take action on my advice.

When I completed my analysis of the data I had gathered over five years in studying the rich and the poor, I realized that wealth and poverty were simply two different systems, or game plans. Those who follow the wealth game plan are able to build wealth. Some, like the O'Neills, even become rich. Those who follow the poverty game plan, like the Veblins, eventually become poor.

The Wealth Game Plan

- Take responsibility for your financial circumstances.
- Improve every day – engage in perpetual, daily self-improvement. Read to learn, not to entertain.
- Pursue your dreams and your goals – do not put your ladder on someone else's wall.
- Set good goals and avoid bad goals – good goals are tied to your dreams and your vision of the ideal person you want to become in the future. Bad goals are goals designed to increase the stuff you own.
- Never quit on your dreams and goals.
- Forge good habits and avoid bad habits – good habits help you become better and move you forward. Bad habits do the opposite.

- Associate with like-minded people who share common, smart money habits. These would be individuals with similar good money habits and who share your financial dreams and goals in life.
- Never gamble.
- Save twenty percent or more of your income first, before spending anything.
- Control your thoughts and emotions.
- Never say what is on your mind – control the words that come out of your mouth.
- Never gossip.
- Seek out mentors who have done what you want to do.
- Never criticize, condemn or complain.
- Exercise every day, aerobically and anaerobically (weight lifting or resistance exercise).
- Eat healthy every day.
- Moderate the bad (eating junk food, watching TV, Internet, drinking alcohol, etc.).
- Live for tomorrow – delay gratification in the pursuit of your dreams and goals.
- Create a clear vision of your ideal, future life – this becomes your new identity and your new behaviors, thoughts, and habits will become the behaviors, thoughts, and habits of the future you.
- Never lie, cheat, or steal.
- Be faithful to your spouse, friends, co-workers, customers, and mentors.
- Meet or exceed expectations others have in you.
- Take educated risks and avoid uneducated risks.

- Experiment until you find your inner talents and devote the rest of your life practicing and perfecting those talents.
- Like or love what you do for a living.
- Provide superior, value-added service or products to others.
- Be a cheerleader not a booleader.
- Become a virtuoso in whatever it is you do for a living.
- Create multiple streams of income – never depend on one stream of income.
- Have a positive, optimistic, success-minded outlook.
- Sleep at least seven hours a day.
- Embrace mistakes/failures – they are your teachers.
- Be frugal with your money.
- Avoid spontaneous or emotional spending.
- Avoid want spending.
- Never supersize your life – don't increase your spending as your income increases.
- Seek happiness in events, not stuff.
- Focus on one task at a time – don't make multi-tasking a habit.
- See wealth as good and poverty as bad.
- Ask for what you want in life.
- Seek feedback from others.
- Never make decisions out of fear.
- Obey and follow laws and rules – there is no shortcut to success.
- Minimize or avoid "do-nothing" habits – these are time-wasting habits that do not help you improve or move you forward in life.

- Patiently pursue your dreams and goals – success takes a long time.
- Treat everyone you meet with respect until they prove they do not deserve it.

The Poverty Game Plan

- Take no responsibility for your life circumstances. Blame everyone but yourself.
- Do not read to learn or for self-improvement – read for entertainment.
- Seek instant gratification.
- Gamble.
- Forge bad habits and "do nothing" habits.
- Spend one hundred percent or more of your income.
- Overextend yourself (i.e. buying or renting a home/ car you can't afford).
- Criticize, condemn, and complain.
- Make decisions out of fear.
- Do not seek out mentors.
- Be afraid to ask for what you want.
- Avoid or ignore feedback.
- Do not challenge yourself – stay within your comfort zone.
- Do not control your thoughts and emotions.
- Say whatever is on your mind – do not control the words that come out of your mouth.
- Associate with like-minded individuals with Poor Money Habits.
- No clear vision of your future.
- Do not pursue dreams and goals.

- Set and pursue bad goals – own a big, expensive home, buy jewelry, purchase or lease luxury cars, go on expensive vacations, etc.
- Quit when the going gets tough.
- Be negative, pessimistic, and cynical about everything.
- Trust no one.
- Gossip.
- Belittle others.
- Be untrustworthy – cheat on your spouse or significant other, backstab friends, colleagues and co-workers.
- Eat in excess.
- Drink alcohol in excess.
- Take recreational drugs in excess.
- Don't exercise consistently.
- Buy whatever you feel like buying immediately and without thinking about the consequences – engage in spontaneous or emotional spending.
- Supersize your life – increase your spending as your income increases.
- Live for today and never plan for your future.
- Fail to meet the expectations of others.
- Ignore laws and rules – lie, cheat and steal in order to shortcut success.

If you were born or raised in poverty, you must change your game plan when you become an adult. Otherwise, poverty will follow you wherever you go. The Wealth Game Plan does not guarantee that you will become a multi-millionaire, but it does guarantee that you will cease being poor.

When the kids were done reading their binders, one by one, they realized JC's seemingly impromptu story about the ONeills and the Veblins was anything but that. The entire beach adventure was a devious, shrewd disguise–a month-long mentorship, dressed up as an exciting beach adventure.

"Totally planned out," Brendan said, as he lifted his eyes to meet JC's.

"Yep," JC replied.

"Were our parents in on it?" Kirsten wanted to know.

"Yep," JC acknowledged.

"I spent a month creating those binders," JC said.

Silence filled the RV. "Look, your parents and I planned this because we love you. This is what I do. People, companies, colleges, schools all pay me a lot of money to share my Rich Habits research. What good is all my knowledge if I can't use that knowledge to help improve the lives of those I love – my family."

"But why not just sit us down for a day or two? Why spend a month visiting New Jersey beaches?" Brendan wondered.

JC pondered the question for a few moments before responding. "Look, learning should be fun. The more fun it is, the more your emotions get involved in the learning process. When your emotions get involved, learning sticks. Plus, you also got to learn, first hand, about our New Jersey beaches. Sure, we could have read about Asbury Park in a book, but isn't it much more fun to experience Asbury Park than to read about it?"

The RV turned the corner onto JC's street in Manasquan. The three grandkids all looked out the RV window as they approached the driveway. Standing in front of JC's house were their parents. To their surprise, standing next to their parents were Tom and Margaret O'Neill. They were all waving and smiling as the RV came to a stop.